The Prompt of It All

(This page intentionally left blank)

The Prompt of It All

Mastering AI Prompt Engineering

By Stephanie L. Carter

The Prompt of It All: Mastering AI Prompt Engineering

Copyright © 2025 by Stephanie L. Carter

Chrysalis Media Pro
Detroit, MI

ISBN: 9798306851051

Printed in United States of America

I dedicate this book to my Lord and Savior, Jesus Christ.

I am profoundly grateful for the love and grounding instilled in me by my parents, Rev. James A. Sr. and Marjorie L. Williams. They gifted me two of the most vital influences in my life: my unwavering faith in Father God and the steadfast support of my big brother, Bishop James A. Williams II. My newest nickname for him, *BishBro* beautifully encapsulates his dual role—my spiritual leader and the ever-watchful protector my mother tasked him to be for his baby sister.

To my husband, Ronnie: Sometimes it feels surreal that more than 30 years have flown by. I am blessed beyond measure that you transitioned from *That Guy* to *My Guy*. I love you, forever and always.

To my heartbeats: Ronnie Jr., Tameka, Nykia, John Robert, Whitley, and Justin—and to their heartbeats: Ronnie III, Ayzia, Cynae, DeYante, DeAngelo, DeJuan, Lathan, Kiara, Zaria, Dominick, Kennedie, Serena, and Feia. I am also deeply thankful for my darling great-grandsons, Logan and King. Whether birthed or bonus, I love you all unconditionally.

To Renee and Tehilla: So many cliffs, so many moments when your voices were the difference between throwing in the towel and taking a "get yourself together" nap before pushing forward. Thank you for your love, patience, listening ears, and comforting words.

And finally, to you, dear reader: Thank you for trusting me to guide you into the world of prompt engineering. Your trust is a gift I cherish deeply. I have poured over every detail in this guide to provide you with the most accurate and helpful information possible. May your Internet journeys be filled with inspiration, and may you create something beautiful and extraordinary.

With love,
Stephanie

Foreword

In a world increasingly driven by artificial intelligence, the art of communicating effectively with machines is more than just a technical skill—it is a bridge to innovation, efficiency, and creativity. "The Prompt of It All" emerges as a beacon for anyone navigating the vast landscape of AI, offering insights into the nuanced interplay between human intent and machine potential.

This book demystifies prompt engineering, equipping readers with tools and techniques to unlock AI's full capabilities. From structuring queries to crafting creative solutions, the content reflects the cutting-edge advancements in technology while remaining accessible to all, regardless of technical background. It is both a guide and an invitation—an invitation to harness the power of AI for personal growth, professional success, and societal impact.

Whether you are a seasoned professional, an educator, a student, or someone simply curious about the future of technology, this book offers something valuable. By mastering the principles outlined here, you are not just learning to work with AI—you are shaping the future of how we interact with intelligent systems.

Dive in, explore, and let "The Prompt of It All" inspire your journey into the transformative world of AI.

Table of Contents

xi

Chapter 1: Introduction to Prompt Engineering

What is Prompt Engineering?

Prompt engineering is the art and science of crafting instructions or queries (prompts) to effectively communicate with AI systems, especially language models like ChatGPT. Think of it as giving precise directions to a highly capable assistant. The quality of a prompt can significantly impact the usefulness, relevance, and clarity of the AI's response.

For example, compare these two prompts:
Poor Prompt: "Tell me about technology."

Effective Prompt: "Explain how advancements in artificial intelligence have impacted healthcare in the past decade, focusing on patient diagnosis and treatment."

The second prompt provides clear instructions, context, and a goal, which leads to a more specific and actionable response.

Why is Prompt Engineering Important?

AI tools are becoming integral to our lives and businesses. They assist with writing, research, decisionmaking, and creative tasks. However, their effectiveness relies on how well we communicate with them. Poorly structured prompts can lead to vague or irrelevant responses, while well-crafted prompts unlock the full potential of AI.

Whether you are writing an email, designing a marketing campaign, or brainstorming ideas for your next project, mastering prompt engineering can make these tasks more efficient and innovative.

The Evolution of AI and the Role of Prompts

Early Days of AI

Artificial intelligence has evolved from rule-based systems that followed strict instructions to modern machine learning models capable of understanding natural language. Early AI required exact, rigid commands far cry from today's conversational systems.

Rise of Language Models

The development of Generative Pre-trained Transformers (GPTs) marked a turning point. GPTs are trained on massive datasets, enabling them to understand and generate human-like text. However, they lack true understanding or intent; they rely entirely on the input provided—your prompt.

Prompts like the Bridge

Prompts are the connection between human intent and machine output. They serve as both the question and the context, guiding the AI toward desired responses. As language models grow more sophisticated, learning to craft precise prompts becomes an invaluable skill.

Applications in Life and Business

Everyday Uses

Personal Productivity: Drafting emails, creating schedules, or generating to-do lists.

Learning and Growth: Summarizing books, explaining complex topics, or tutoring new skills.

Creativity: Writing stories, brainstorming ideas, or composing music.

Business Applications

Customer Support: Automating responses to frequently asked questions.

Marketing: Generating ad copy, social media posts, and content strategies.

Decision-Making: Analyzing data trends, conducting SWOT analyses, and forecasting.

By learning prompt engineering, you can enhance your personal productivity and gain a competitive edge in your career or business.

Why This Skill is Critical Today

Ubiquity of AI

AI is no longer confined to tech giants. Tools like ChatGPT are accessible to individuals, small businesses, and educators. They are being used across industries, including healthcare, finance, education, and entertainment.

Staying Competitive

Understanding AI tools and leveraging their capabilities is becoming a core competency. Just as knowing how to use a computer was revolutionary in the 1990s, prompt engineering is essential in the AI-driven world.

Prompt engineering empowers individuals, regardless of technical expertise, to access and utilize AI effectively. This levels the playing field, enabling more people to innovate and solve problems creatively.

Exercises to Get Started

Exercise 1: Exploring Basic Prompts

Write a prompt to summarize a recent news article. Use this structure:

Context: What is the article about?

Instruction: What should the AI do?

Goal: What is the desired outcome?

Experiment with the same query but vary the level of detail in your prompts. Note how the responses change.

Exercise 2: Refining Clarity
Write a vague prompt like: "Tell me something interesting."
Rewrite it to be more specific: "Share a surprising fact about the

history of space exploration." Compare the results and identify why the

second prompt was more effective.

Conclusion

Prompt engineering is a powerful skill that bridges human creativity and AI capabilities. By mastering this foundational tool, you can unlock new levels of productivity, innovation, and problem-solving in both your personal and professional life. In the next chapter, we'll delve deeper into understanding AI and language models, providing the context needed to craft even better prompts.

Chapter 2: Understanding AI and Language Models

Basics of AI and How Language Models Work

Artificial Intelligence (AI) is the simulation of human intelligence by machines. While AI spans a broad spectrum, this chapter focuses on language models—systems designed to understand, generate, and interact using human language. To harness their full potential, it's essential to grasp the foundational concepts.

What Are Language Models?

Language models, such as Generative Pre-trained Transformers (GPTs), are specialized AI systems trained on vast amounts of text data. Their primary task is to predict the next word in a sequence, enabling them to generate coherent and contextually relevant responses. For instance:

Input: "The sky is..."

Output: "blue and clear today."

While this may seem simple, the underlying mechanisms involve complex computations and immense datasets.

How Do Language Models Work?

Training on Large Datasets

Language models are trained on diverse text sources, including books, websites, and articles. This equips them with a broad understanding of language patterns and structures.

Tokenization

Text is broken into smaller units, called tokens. For example, the sentence "AI is amazing" becomes ["AI," "is," "amazing"].

Contextual Understanding

Models analyze the context of words. For example, the word "bank" might refer to a financial institution or a riverbank, depending on the surrounding words.

Generating Responses

When prompted, the model uses its training to predict and generate the most likely sequence of words based on the input.

Strengths of Language Models

Versatility: They can perform a wide range of tasks, from answering questions to writing poetry.

Speed: They process and generate information faster than most humans.

Adaptability: With the right prompts, they can be tailored to various applications.

Limitations of Language Models

Lack of True Understanding: Language models don't comprehend text like humans. They generate responses based on patterns, not intent or meaning.

Dependence on Data: Biases in training data can lead to biased outputs.

Vulnerability to Ambiguity: Poorly structured prompts can result in vague or irrelevant responses.

Context, Syntax, and Semantics in Prompts

Effective prompting relies on three core elements: context, syntax, and semantics. Understanding these components helps in crafting precise and effective queries.

Context

Context provides the background or setting for the prompt. It ensures that the AI understands what the user is asking and why.

Weak Context: "Explain photosynthesis."

Strong Context: "Explain photosynthesis to a 10-year-old using simple language."

Syntax

Syntax refers to the grammatical structure of the prompt. Clear syntax ensures that the AI interprets the request correctly.

Poor Syntax: "What are photosynthesis process explain?"

Good Syntax: "Explain the process of photosynthesis."

Semantics

Semantics deals with the meaning behind the words. Precise semantics ensure that the prompt conveys the user's intent.

Ambiguous: "Describe the bank."

Specific: "Describe the financial operations of a bank."

Limitations and Strengths of AI in Response Generation

While AI can be a powerful ally, understanding its strengths and limitations helps manage expectations and maximize effectiveness.

Strengths

Efficiency: AI can process and analyze vast amounts of data in seconds.

Consistency: Unlike humans, AI doesn't suffer from fatigue or mood swings.

Creativity: AI can generate ideas, stories, and solutions that humans might not consider.

Limitations

No True Intelligence: AI lacks self-awareness, emotions, and genuine understanding.

Bias: AI can inadvertently reflect biases present in its training data.

Dependence on User Input: The quality of AI responses hinges on the clarity and precision of the prompts provided.

Exercises to Reinforce Learning

Exercise 1: Analyzing Context, Syntax, and Semantics

Write a prompt with weak context, syntax, and semantics. For example: "Explain it better."

Rewrite the prompt to enhance each element. For example: "Explain the benefits of renewable energy to someone unfamiliar with the topic."

Compare the AI's responses to see how improvements in the prompt affect the output.

Exercise 2: Exploring AI Strengths and Limitations

Provide an open-ended prompt, such as: "Generate a creative story about a robot learning emotions."

Provide a highly specific prompt, such as: "Write a 500-word story about a robot in the year 2050 discovering emotions after rescuing a cat."

Compare the two responses and identify the model's strengths and weaknesses.

Conclusion

Understanding how AI and language models work is crucial for effective prompt engineering. By mastering the interplay between context, syntax, and semantics, you can craft prompts that maximize AI's potential while navigating its limitations. In the next chapter, we'll explore the psychology behind prompts and how they mimic human communication, unlocking new strategies for interaction.

Chapter 3: The Psychology of Prompts

How Prompts Mimic Human Communication

Human communication relies on clarity, intent, and shared understanding. When interacting with AI, prompts serve as the primary mechanism to replicate these elements. Understanding how prompts mimic human communication can help refine their construction and improve the results obtained from AI.

Intent and Purpose:

In a conversation, we clarify our goals. Similarly, prompts need clear intent.

Example: Asking a friend, "Can you help me write a letter?" translates to an AI prompt like, "Draft a formal letter requesting a job interview."

Context and Framing:

Just as context in a discussion shapes understanding, context in prompts guides AI responses.

Example: Providing a backstory in a prompt ensures relevant AI-generated content.

Adjusting for the Audience:

Tailoring communication to the listener parallels structuring prompts for AI's specific capabilities.

Example: Speaking simply to a child vs. asking AI to "explain photosynthesis in basic terms."

Challenges of Mimicking Human Communication

AI lacks emotions and true comprehension, relying solely on patterns.

Miscommunication occurs when prompts are ambiguous or overly complex, just as unclear language causes confusion in human interactions.

Leveraging Cognitive Patterns in Effective Prompting

Human cognition is influenced by familiarity, structure, and relevance. Prompts that align with these cognitive patterns tend to yield better responses.

Familiarity and Pattern Recognition

AI excels at recognizing patterns, and leveraging familiar structures can improve outcomes.

Example: Instead of asking, "How do trees work?" use a structured question: "Explain the process of photosynthesis in plants."

Hierarchical Thinking

Humans often process information hierarchically, moving from general to specific. Prompts that follow this flow are easier for AI to process effectively.

Example:

General: "Describe renewable energy."
Specific: "Focus on solar energy and its applications in residential settings."

Anchoring with Context

Providing anchors, or reference points, helps AI generate precise and relevant responses.

Example: "Using examples from the last decade, discuss how technology has transformed education."

The Role of Specificity and Clarity in Communication

Specificity and clarity are critical in human interactions and equally essential when crafting prompts. Ambiguity leads to confusion, while precision ensures understanding and alignment.

Why Specificity Matters

Specific prompts reduce ambiguity and guide the AI's focus.
Ambiguous: "Tell me about marketing."

Specific: "Explain how digital marketing strategies differ from traditional marketing, using social media as an example."

The Importance of Clarity

Clear prompts avoid misinterpretation and ensure the AI delivers accurate results.
Unclear: "What about climate change?"

Clear: "Provide an overview of the causes and effects of climate change, focusing on rising global temperatures."

Balancing Specificity and Flexibility

While specificity is essential, overly rigid prompts can limit creativity. Striking a balance allows AI to offer diverse and valuable insights.

Example:
Too Rigid: "List 10 advantages of solar panels only for suburban homes."

Balanced: "Discuss the advantages of solar panels for residential use, highlighting diverse settings."

Exercises to Enhance Prompting Skills

Exercise 1: Practicing Clarity
Write a vague prompt, such as: "What's the deal with exercise?"

Rewrite the prompt to improve clarity: "Explain the benefits of regular exercise on mental and physical health."
Compare the AI's responses to assess the impact of clarity.

Exercise 2: Exploring Cognitive Anchors
Write a prompt that provides minimal context: "Talk about history."

Add cognitive anchors: "Describe the key events of the American Revolution and their impact on modern democracy."
Evaluate how the added context changes the AI's response.

Exercise 3: Balancing Specificity and Flexibility
Create an overly rigid prompt: "List 5 uses of AI in marketing campaigns for clothing brands."
Revise to allow more creativity: "Explore how AI can enhance marketing

strategies in the fashion industry." Analyze the variety and depth of the

responses.

Conclusion

Prompts are the bridge between human intention and AI capability, mimicking the intricacies of human communication. By understanding cognitive patterns and prioritizing specificity and clarity, you can craft prompts that elicit meaningful and accurate responses. As we move to the next chapter, we'll explore the anatomy of a good prompt, diving deeper into the building blocks of effective prompting.

Chapter 4: The Anatomy of a Good Prompt

Key Components: Context, Instruction, and Goal

Crafting a good prompt requires understanding its three core components: context, instruction, and goal. Each plays a crucial role in shaping the quality of the AI's response.

Context: Setting the Stage

Context provides the background or setting for the prompt, ensuring the AI understands the situation or subject. It anchors the response, making it relevant and coherent.

Example Without Context: "Explain photosynthesis."

Example With Context: "Explain photosynthesis to a group of fifth graders learning about plant biology for the first time."

Instruction: Defining the Task

Clear instructions tell the AI what you expect. Vague instructions lead to vague answers, while specific instructions guide the AI toward desired outputs.

Vague Instruction: "Tell me something about health."

Clear Instruction: "List five benefits of regular physical exercise for cardiovascular health."

Goal: Clarifying the Desired Outcome

The goal specifies what the user wants to achieve with the AI's response. It ensures that the output aligns with the user's expectations.

Without Goal: "Discuss renewable energy."

With Goal: "Provide an overview of renewable energy, focusing on its environmental and economic benefits."

Balancing Conciseness with Detail

A good prompt strikes a balance between being concise and providing enough detail. Overly long prompts can confuse the AI, while overly brief ones lack the information needed for accurate responses.

Tips for Conciseness and Detail

Be Direct: Remove unnecessary words or phrases.

Wordy: "Can you please, if it's not too much trouble, list the main causes of climate change?"

Concise: "List the main causes of climate change."

Include Relevant Details: Add specifics that guide the response.

Vague: "Explain marketing strategies."

Detailed: "Explain effective digital marketing strategies for small businesses on a tight budget." Avoid Overloading: Don't cram too many instructions into a single prompt.

Overloaded: "Explain marketing strategies, list examples, and summarize key trends for the last five years." Focused: "Explain effective digital marketing strategies for small businesses."

Common Mistakes and How to Avoid Them

Mistake 1: Ambiguity

Ambiguous prompts lead to unclear or irrelevant responses.
Example: "Tell me about AI."
The AI might discuss AI's history, applications, or challenges. Adding specificity avoids this issue.
Solution: "Provide an overview of AI's role in healthcare, focusing on diagnostic tools."

Mistake 2: Over-Complexity

Overly complex prompts confuse the AI and reduce the quality of the response.

Example: "Explain AI in healthcare, its advantages, disadvantages, historical development, and future potential."

This overwhelms the AI with multiple tasks.

Solution: Break it into smaller prompts:
"Explain AI's advantages in healthcare."
"Discuss the challenges of AI in healthcare."

Mistake 3: Lack of Focus

Prompts without a clear goal can result in generic or unfocused answers.
Example: "Discuss marketing."

The AI may produce an overly broad response.
Solution: "Discuss how social media marketing can increase brand awareness for startups."

Exercises to Practice Prompt Crafting

Exercise 1: Refining Ambiguous Prompts
Start with a vague prompt, such as: "What is AI?"

Rewrite it to include context, instruction, and a goal: "Explain what artificial intelligence is, focusing on its impact on the education sector."
Compare the AI's responses to assess improvement.

Exercise 2: Balancing Conciseness and Detail

Write an overly detailed prompt: "Explain the benefits of exercise, list specific examples, discuss its impact on mental health, and compare aerobic and anaerobic activities."
Simplify it: "Explain the benefits of exercise, focusing

on mental health." Observe the difference in responses.

Exercise 3: Breaking Down Overloaded Prompts
Take a complex prompt: "Describe renewable energy, its types,

applications, and future trends." Break it into smaller prompts:

"Describe the main types of renewable energy."
"Discuss the applications of renewable energy in urban areas."
"Explain future trends in renewable energy

development." Analyze the clarity and depth

of the outputs.

Conclusion

The anatomy of a good prompt lies in its structure: context, instruction, and goal. Balancing conciseness with detail and avoiding common mistakes ensures high-quality AI responses. By practicing these techniques, you can refine your prompting skills and unlock the full potential of AI tools. In the next chapter, we'll explore different types and structures of prompts, expanding your toolkit for various scenarios.

Chapter 5: Prompt Types and Structures

Understanding different prompt types and their structures is crucial for mastering prompt engineering. This chapter explores various types of prompts, their use cases, and how to structure them for optimal results.

Open-Ended vs. Closed-Ended Prompts
Open-Ended Prompts

Open-ended prompts encourage expansive, creative, or exploratory responses. These prompts are useful for brainstorming, storytelling, and idea generation.

Example: "What are some innovative ways to use renewable

energy in urban settings?" Benefits

Encourages diverse responses.

Sparks creativity and exploration.

Challenges

May produce responses that are too broad or unfocused.

Closed-Ended Prompts

Closed-ended prompts guide the AI toward specific, concise answers. These are ideal for factual queries or tasks requiring precision.

Example: "List three advantages of solar energy."

Benefits

Provides clear, targeted responses.

Saves time when precision is critical.

Challenges

Limits creativity and depth.

Choosing Between Open and Closed Prompts

Use open-ended prompts when exploring possibilities or seeking innovative ideas. Opt for closed-ended prompts when clarity and specificity are more important.

Instructional Prompts vs. Creative Prompts
Instructional Prompts

Instructional prompts give clear, actionable directions to complete a specific task. These are effective for generating structured outputs such as summaries, lists, or instructions.

Example: "Summarize the main points of this article on climate change."

Best Practices

Be specific about the desired format and content.

Provide additional context if needed.

Creative Prompts

Creative prompts encourage the AI to produce imaginative and original responses. These are ideal for tasks like storytelling, poetry, or designing slogans.

Example: "Write a short story about a robot discovering emotions."

Best Practices

Set boundaries for the creative output, such as length or tone.

Use open-ended language to inspire creativity.

Combining Instructional and Creative Prompts

You can blend these approaches to achieve specific yet creative outcomes.

Example: "Write a humorous advertisement for a solar-powered phone charger."

Multi-Step Prompts for Complex Outputs

What Are Multi-Step Prompts?

Multi-step prompts break down a complex task into smaller, sequential steps. This structure guides the AI through a logical progression, improving clarity and coherence.

Example:
"List the main causes of climate change."
"Explain how each cause contributes to global warming."
"Suggest actionable steps individuals can take to mitigate these causes."

Benefits of Multi-Step Prompts

Improves the depth and quality of responses.

Makes complex tasks manageable and organized.

Crafting Multi-Step Prompts

Identify the Goal: Define the end result you want.

Break It Down: Divide the task into clear, logical steps.

Sequence the Steps: Ensure each step builds on the previous one.

Example: Writing a Research Report
"Provide an overview of the topic."
"List the key challenges associated with this topic."
"Summarize potential solutions with supporting examples."

Exercises to Practice Prompt Structuring

Exercise 1: Open-Ended vs. Closed-Ended Prompts

Write an open-ended prompt: "Describe the future of electric vehicles."

Rewrite it as a closed-ended prompt: "List three trends shaping the future of electric vehicles."

Compare the AI's responses to understand the difference in depth and focus.

Exercise 2: Instructional and Creative Prompts

Write an instructional prompt: "Explain how to bake a chocolate cake."

Write a creative prompt: "Invent a story about a magical chocolate cake that grants wishes."

Blend the two: "Write a whimsical recipe for a chocolate cake that grants wishes."

Exercise 3: Multi-Step Prompts

Start with a complex task: "Explain the benefits of

renewable energy." Break it into steps:

"List the main types of renewable energy."
"Describe the environmental benefits of each type."
"Provide examples of countries effectively using

renewable energy." Evaluate how step-by-step

prompts enhance clarity.

Conclusion

Understanding and applying different prompt types and structures is essential for effective prompt engineering. Open-ended and closed-ended prompts, instructional and creative approaches, and multi-step structures provide flexibility and precision. In the next chapter, we'll explore how to refine and iterate on prompts to achieve even better results.

Chapter 6: Iterative Prompting and Refinement

The Importance of Refining Prompts

No prompt is perfect on the first try. Iterative prompting involves testing, analyzing, and improving prompts to ensure they produce the best possible responses. Refinement transforms vague or ineffective queries into precise tools for extracting value from AI.

Why Refinement Matters

Improves Accuracy: A refined prompt delivers more relevant and specific responses.

Enhances Clarity: Clear prompts minimize confusion and ambiguity.

Refines Efficiency: Iterative refinement reduces the need for repeated corrections or clarifications.

How to Test and Refine Prompts

Step 1: Analyze Initial Responses

Start with a basic prompt and evaluate the AI's output for relevance, accuracy, and completeness.

Example: Prompt: "Tell me about renewable energy."

Response: "Renewable energy comes from sources that are naturally replenished, such as solar, wind, and hydro."

Analysis: The response is right but lacks depth and specifics.

Step 2: Identify Weaknesses

Look for:

Lack of Specificity: Is the response too general?

Irrelevance: Does the output stray from the intended topic?

Incompleteness: Are critical points missing?

Step 3: Refine the Prompt

Adjust the prompt to address these weaknesses. Add context, clarify instructions, or specify goals.

Refined Prompt: "Explain the environmental benefits of renewable energy, focusing on solar and wind power."

Expected Response: "Solar and wind energy reduce greenhouse gas emissions by replacing fossil fuels. They also decrease air pollution and lower water usage in energy production."

Step 4: Iterate

Repeat the process, refining the prompt further until the response meets your needs. Each iteration brings you closer to the ideal prompt.

Techniques for Refining Prompts

Use Specific Language

Specificity reduces ambiguity and ensures the AI focuses on the intended topic.

Vague: "What is AI?"

Specific: "Provide a brief overview of artificial intelligence, including its applications in healthcare and education."

Provide Context

Context helps the AI understand the background or purpose of the query.

Without Context: "Explain photosynthesis."

With Context: "Explain photosynthesis to a 10-year-old learning about plant biology."

Ask for Examples

Examples enrich the response and make it more actionable.

Without Examples: "Explain renewable energy."

With Examples: "Explain renewable energy, including examples like solar panels and wind turbines."

Specify Format

Defining the format of the response ensures clarity and usability.

No Format Specified: "List the benefits of exercise."

Format Specified: "List five benefits of exercise in bullet points."

Use Step-by-Step Prompts

Breaking complex tasks into steps improves coherence.

Single-Step: "Describe climate change and its

impact."

Multi-Step:

"Define climate change."

"Explain its primary causes."

"Describe its effects on the environment and human health."

Identifying and Addressing Vague Responses

Sometimes, even refined prompts yield vague or incomplete answers. Here's how to address them:

Strategy 1: Probe for Details
Example Response: "AI helps in many industries."
Follow-Up Prompt: "Which industries benefit most from AI, and how?"

Strategy 2: Rephrase for Clarity
Initial Prompt: "Explain renewable energy."

Rephrased Prompt: "Provide a detailed explanation of renewable energy, focusing on solar and wind power technologies."

Strategy 3: Narrow the Scope
Broad Prompt: "Discuss technology in education."
Refined Prompt: "Explain how technology enhances personalized learning in K-12 education."

Exercises to Practice Iterative Prompting

Exercise 1: Refining for Specificity
Start with a vague prompt:

"Explain AI." Refine it iteratively:

"Explain AI applications in healthcare."
"Explain how AI improves diagnostic accuracy

in healthcare." Compare the responses at each

step.

Exercise 2: Adding Context
Write a basic prompt: "What is photosynthesis?"
Add context: "What is photosynthesis, and why is it important for plants?"
Further refine: "Explain photosynthesis to a middle school student,

emphasizing its role in the food chain." Exercise 3: Specifying Format

Start with an open prompt: "List benefits of exercise."
Refine with format: "List five benefits of exercise in bullet points."

Add audience context: "List five benefits of exercise for office workers in bullet points."

Conclusion

Iterative prompting and refinement are essential for effective communication with AI. By testing and improving your prompts, you can achieve precise, relevant, and actionable responses. In the next chapter, we'll explore how to apply prompt engineering techniques to personal productivity and goal setting.

Chapter 7: Personal Productivity and Goal Setting

Using Prompts for Task Management and Prioritization

AI-powered tools can transform how we manage tasks and set priorities. By crafting effective prompts, you can streamline your workflow and focus on what truly matters.

Task Management with Prompts

Prompts can help you break down large projects into manageable tasks, create schedules, and track progress.

Example Prompt: "Create a weekly schedule for completing a 10-page research paper, breaking the work into daily tasks."

AI Response:

Monday: Research and outline sections 1 and 2.

Tuesday: Write a draft of section 1.

Wednesday: Write a draft of section 2, and so on.

Prioritizing Tasks

Prompts can aid in evaluating which tasks are most critical based on deadlines, importance, or impact.

Example Prompt: "Prioritize these tasks based on urgency and importance: responding to emails, preparing for a meeting, completing a report, and organizing files." AI Response:

Completing the report (high urgency and importance).

Preparing for the meeting (important but less urgent).

Responding to emails (urgent but less important).

Organizing files (low urgency and importance).

Enhancing Decision-Making with AI Assistance

AI can act as a virtual advisor, offering perspectives, weighing pros and cons, and offering data-driven insights.

Decision-Making Scenarios

Weighing Options:

Prompt: "List the pros and cons of purchasing an electric vehicle versus a hybrid vehicle." AI Response:

Electric Vehicle Pros: Zero emissions, lower operating costs.

Electric Vehicle Cons: Higher upfront cost, limited charging infrastructure.

Hybrid Vehicle Pros: Greater range, lower upfront cost.

Hybrid Vehicle Cons: Higher emissions compared to electric vehicles.

Risk Assessment:

Prompt: "Assess the risks of launching a new

product in Q4 versus Q1." AI Response:

Q4 Risks: Market saturation due to holiday season, shorter launch window.

Q1 Risks: Lower consumer spending post-holidays, reduced promotional opportunities.

Building Confidence in Decisions

By using AI to simulate scenarios or analyze data, you can approach decisions with greater clarity and confidence.

Designing Prompts for Brainstorming and Ideation

AI excels at generating ideas, making it an invaluable tool for brainstorming sessions. Well-crafted prompts can unlock creativity and expand possibilities.

Generating Ideas

Prompt: "Suggest innovative marketing strategies for a small bakery

looking to attract local customers." AI Response:

Host a community bake-off.

Offer discounts for referrals.

Collaborate with local coffee shops.

Introduce a seasonal menu.

Exploring Alternatives

Prompt: "What are alternative uses for a

vacant lot in an urban area?" AI Response:

Community garden.

Pop-up event space.

Outdoor art gallery.

Fitness and wellness park.

Refining Ideas

AI can also help refine initial ideas by focusing on feasibility or aligning them with specific goals.

Prompt: "How can the idea of a community bake-off be

adapted for an online audience?" AI Response:

Organize a virtual baking competition via social media.

Offer prizes for the best photos or recipes submitted online.

Partner with influencers to judge entries.

Exercises to Practice Productivity Prompts

Exercise 1: Breaking Down a Goal
Write a goal: "Write a book in six months."

Craft a prompt to create a timeline: "Develop a six-month plan to write a 300-page book, including research, drafting, and editing phases."
Refine the timeline based on the AI's suggestions.

Exercise 2: Prioritizing Tasks
List tasks: "Prepare a presentation, respond to emails, finish a report, and clean the workspace."
Write a prompt: "Prioritize these tasks based on a deadline of 3 PM today."
Compare the AI's prioritization with your instincts.

Exercise 3: Brainstorming Solutions
Identify a challenge: "Increase attendance at a community event."
Write a prompt: "Suggest creative strategies to attract more

attendees to a local event." Evaluate the AI's suggestions and

select the most workable ideas.

Conclusion

Prompt engineering for personal productivity and goal setting allows you to leverage AI as a powerful ally in managing tasks, making decisions, and generating ideas. By crafting thoughtful prompts, you can maximize efficiency and creativity in your daily life. In the next chapter, we'll explore how to use prompts for learning and skill development, further expanding your toolkit for personal growth.

Chapter 8: Prompting for Learning and Skill Development

Generating Study Guides and Educational Materials

AI can assist in creating personalized study plans, summaries, and educational resources tailored to your learning needs. Well-crafted prompts can help you absorb knowledge efficiently and effectively.

Creating Study Plans

AI can break down complex topics into manageable sections and suggest timelines for mastering them.

Example Prompt: "Create a one-month study plan for learning the basics of Python programming." AI Response:

Week 1: Learn basic syntax, variables, and data types.

Week 2: Explore loops and conditional statements.

Week 3: Understand functions and modules.

Week 4: Practice with small projects.

Summarizing Information

AI can generate concise summaries of articles, books, or lectures, highlighting key points.

Example Prompt: "Summarize the main arguments of the book 'Atomic Habits' by James Clear." AI Response:

Small habits lead to significant change over time.

Focus on identity-based habits for sustainable results.

Build habits using cues, cravings, responses, and rewards.

Designing Flashcards and Quizzes

Prompts can be used to create learning tools such as flashcards and quizzes for self-assessment.

Example Prompt: "Create five flashcards about the solar system for a middle school student." AI Response:

Question: What is the largest planet in the solar system? Answer: Jupiter.

Question: Which planet is closest to the sun? Answer: Mercury.

Question: What is the name of Earth's natural satellite? Answer: The Moon.

Interactive Learning Through Effective Questioning

Asking questions is a fundamental way to learn. AI can simulate interactive learning environments, providing explanations and answering queries in real-time.

Exploring Topics with Guided Questions

Prompt: "Explain how photosynthesis works, focusing on the role of chlorophyll."

AI Response: "Photosynthesis is the process by which plants convert sunlight into energy. Chlorophyll, found in plant cells, absorbs sunlight and uses its energy to synthesize glucose from carbon dioxide and water."

Using Follow-Up Prompts

You can refine your understanding by asking follow-up questions.
Initial Prompt: "What is the role of chlorophyll in photosynthesis?"
Follow-Up Prompt: "Why is chlorophyll green?"

AI Response: "Chlorophyll appears green because it absorbs red and blue light wavelengths while reflecting green light."

Simulating Real-Life Scenarios

AI can act as a tutor, role-playing scenarios to enhance learning.
Prompt: "Pretend to be a job interviewer asking questions

about project management skills." AI Response:

"Can you describe a time when you managed a project under a tight deadline?"
"How do you prioritize tasks in a complex project?"

Personal Growth: Prompts for Reflection and Journaling

Reflection is a powerful tool for personal growth. AI can guide you through reflective practices and journaling to help clarify thoughts, set goals, and evaluate progress.

Reflective Prompts

Prompt: "What are three things you learned from

your most recent challenge?" AI Response:

Importance of adaptability.

Value of seeking help when needed.

Recognizing progress despite setbacks.

Goal-Setting Prompts

Prompt: "Help me set SMART goals for

improving my fitness." AI Response:

Specific: "Run 5 kilometers without stopping."
Measurable: "Track distance and time using a fitness app."
Achievable: "Start with 2 kilometers and gradually increase."
Relevant: "Improve cardiovascular health."
Time-bound: "Achieve this within 8 weeks."

Guided Journaling

AI can provide journaling prompts to encourage introspection and mindfulness.

Prompt: "What are three things you are

grateful for today, and why?" AI Response:

Grateful for good health because it enables productivity.

Grateful for supportive friends who provide encouragement.

Grateful for a sunny day, which boosts mood and energy.

Exercises for Learning and Skill Development

Exercise 1: Crafting Study Prompts
Choose a topic: "Learn about the French Revolution."
Write a prompt: "Summarize the causes and key events of the French Revolution."
Evaluate the AI's response and refine the prompt for more detail or focus.

Exercise 2: Interactive Questions
Start with a broad question: "What is

climate change?" Follow up with specific

prompts:

"What are the primary causes of climate change?"
"How does climate change affect biodiversity?"

Use the responses to deepen your understanding.

Exercise 3: Reflective Journaling

Write a reflective prompt: "What did I achieve this week, and how can I improve next week?" Review the AI's suggestions and incorporate them into your journaling practice.

Conclusion

Prompts for learning and skill development empower you to create personalized educational experiences, foster interactive learning, and support personal growth through reflection and journaling. In the next chapter, we'll explore how to use prompts for creative problem-solving, helping you tackle challenges with innovative approaches.

Chapter 9: Creative Problem-Solving

Crafting Prompts for Innovation and Solutions

AI can serve as a powerful ally in solving complex problems and fostering innovation. The key lies in crafting prompts that encourage creative and practical solutions.

Encouraging Divergent Thinking

Divergent thinking involves generating multiple solutions to a problem. Prompts that encourage exploration and brainstorming can unlock AI's potential for innovation.

Example Prompt: "Suggest 10 unique ways to reduce

plastic waste in urban areas." AI Response:

Install vending machines that dispense reusable containers.

Incentivize shops to offer discounts for using personal bags.

Introduce municipal plastic exchange programs.

Framing Problems Effectively

The way a problem is framed affects the quality of the solutions.
Vague Prompt: "How can we solve global warming?"

Refined Prompt: "What are five actionable steps that urban planners can take to reduce greenhouse gas emissions?"

Encouraging Constraints

Adding constraints to prompts fosters creativity by narrowing the focus and challenging the AI to think within boundaries.

Example Prompt: "Design a community park with a budget of $50,000, emphasizing sustainability and low maintenance."

AI Response:

Use recycled materials for benches and pathways.

Incorporate drought-resistant plants.

Build a small solar-powered water feature.

AI as a Collaborator in Creative Fields

AI can act as a virtual collaborator, providing ideas, refining concepts, and generating drafts for creative projects.

Writing and Storytelling

Prompt: "Write the opening paragraph of a novel about a detective solving a mystery in a futuristic city."

AI Response: "In the neon-lit sprawl of New Haven City, Detective Mira Cassini navigated shadows and secrets. Tonight, a whisper of danger lingered in the air, carried by the hum of levitating taxis and the flicker of holographic billboards."

Visual Design

AI tools can assist in generating ideas for logos, illustrations, and layouts.

Prompt: "Suggest three concepts for a logo representing a sustainable fashion brand." AI Response:

A minimalist leaf design interwoven with a hanger.

A stylized globe made of fabric swatches.

A needle and thread forming the infinity symbol.

Music and Sound Design

Prompt: "Compose a 30-second jingle for an eco-friendly cleaning product."

AI Response: "Start with an upbeat acoustic guitar riff, add cheerful lyrics about freshness and green living, and finish with a catchy chorus."

Overcoming Creative Blocks with Targeted Prompting

When creativity stalls, AI can provide inspiration and reignite momentum by suggesting ideas or offering fresh perspectives.

Generating Fresh Perspectives

Prompt: "What are unconventional ways to market a book about personal finance?" AI Response:

Host a webinar series featuring unique money-saving challenges.

Create a social media campaign where followers share their financial success stories.

Develop interactive quizzes to determine financial personalities.

Expanding on Existing Ideas

Initial Idea: "Create an app for stress management."

Prompt: "Suggest features for a stress management app aimed at working professionals." AI Response:

Guided meditation sessions tailored to work schedules.

Daily affirmations and stress-relief tips.

Progress tracking with mood analytics.

Breaking Down Complex Problems

Problem: "Our team struggles with collaboration on remote projects."
Prompt: "List tools and strategies to improve remote team collaboration and communication." AI Response:

Implement project management software like Trello or Asana.

Schedule regular video check-ins to maintain team alignment.

Use collaborative tools like Miro for brainstorming sessions.

Exercises to Practice Creative Problem-Solving Prompts

Exercise 1: Divergent Thinking
Write a broad problem: "How can a small town attract more tourists?"

Craft a prompt: "Suggest 10 innovative ways for a small town to attract tourists, focusing on cultural events and local businesses."
Review the AI's suggestions and identify the most feasible ideas.
Exercise 2: Collaborative Creativity
Identify a creative project: "Design a poster for a charity run."

Write a prompt: "Generate three design concepts for a poster advertising a charity run, emphasizing health and community."
Evaluate the AI's concepts and refine them.

Exercise 3: Overcoming Creative Blocks
State a challenge: "I'm stuck on naming a new eco-friendly product line."

Write a prompt: "Suggest five names for an eco-friendly product line focused on sustainable cleaning solutions."

Use the suggestions as inspiration.

Conclusion

AI-driven prompts for creative problem-solving enable you to approach challenges with fresh perspectives, overcome blocks, and innovate effectively. By crafting thoughtful prompts, you can unlock AI's potential as a collaborator in generating ideas and solutions. In the next chapter, we'll explore how to apply these techniques to customer interaction and support, extending their utility into business applications.

Chapter 10: Customer Interaction and Support

Designing Prompts for Chatbots and Virtual Assistants

AI-powered chatbots and virtual assistants are transforming customer interaction by providing instant, accurate, and scalable support. Effective prompt design is essential for creating systems that address customer needs efficiently and empathetically.

Understanding Customer Intent

A well-crafted prompt anticipates the customer's intent and guides the AI to provide relevant responses.

Example Prompt: "If a customer asks about the return policy, respond with a detailed explanation, including conditions and time frames."

AI Response: "Our return policy allows returns within 30 days of purchase with a valid receipt. Items must be unused and in their original packaging."

Providing Contextual Responses

Incorporate context to personalize interactions.

Customer Query: "Where is my order?"

Prompt: "If a customer asks about order status, request their order number and provide an estimated delivery time based on the tracking system."

AI Response: "Could you provide your order number? I can then check the estimated delivery date for you."

Ensuring Clarity and Tone

The AI's tone should align with the brand's voice and be clear to avoid misunderstandings.

Prompt for Tone: "Respond to all customer queries in a friendly, professional tone, avoiding technical jargon."

Managing FAQs and Troubleshooting

AI can automate responses to frequently asked questions (FAQs) and assist in troubleshooting common issues, saving time and resources.

Automating FAQs

Create specific prompts to address common inquiries.

Example Prompt: "If a customer asks about store hours, provide the weekday and weekend schedules."

AI Response: "Our store is open Monday through Friday from 9 AM to 9 PM and on weekends from 10 AM to 6 PM."

Step-by-Step Troubleshooting
AI can guide users through problem-solving processes by breaking down solutions into steps.

Customer Query: "My internet isn't working."

Prompt: "Guide the customer through troubleshooting their internet connection, starting with checking the modem and router." AI Response:

"Ensure your modem and router are powered on."
"Check if all cables are securely connected."
"Restart your modem and router."

Enhancing User Experience Through Prompt Optimization
Effective prompts not only resolve customer issues but also enhance their overall experience by making interactions smooth and efficient.

Personalizing Responses
Personalization fosters trust and improves customer satisfaction.

Prompt: "Address the customer by their name when it's provided in the query."

AI Response: "Thank you for reaching out, John. How can I assist you today?"

Offering Proactive Assistance
Anticipate follow-up questions to provide comprehensive answers.

Customer Query: "How do I reset my password?"

Prompt: "Explain the steps to reset a password and include a link to the password reset page."

AI Response: "To reset your password, click on the 'Forgot Password' link on the login page. Enter your registered email address to receive a reset link."

Streamlining Escalations
AI can identify when an issue requires human intervention and escalate appropriately.

Prompt: "If a customer query cannot be resolved in three responses, escalate the issue to a human representative."

AI Response: "I'm escalating your issue to one of our support specialists who will assist you further."

Exercises to Practice Customer Interaction Prompts
Exercise 1: Writing FAQ Prompts

Identify a common question: "What is your shipping policy?"

Write a prompt: "Respond to shipping policy inquiries with details about delivery times, costs, and international shipping options."
Test the AI's response and refine as needed.

Exercise 2: Crafting Troubleshooting Prompts
State a problem: "The app is not loading."
Write a prompt: "Guide the customer through basic

troubleshooting steps for app issues." Evaluate the response

for clarity and effectiveness. Exercise 3: Enhancing User

Experience

Write a prompt to personalize interactions: "If a customer provides their name, address them by it in the response."
Test the AI's ability to incorporate personalization seamlessly.

Conclusion

Effective prompt engineering for customer interaction and support improves efficiency, satisfaction, and scalability. By crafting prompts that anticipate customer needs, deliver clear responses, and enhance personalization, businesses can elevate their support systems. The next chapter will explore how to use AI-driven prompts for marketing and content creation, further expanding its business applications.

Chapter 11: Marketing and Content Creation

Generating Engaging Headlines, Posts, and Ads

AI tools can help businesses craft compelling marketing materials that capture attention and drive engagement. Prompts designed for marketing must be precise, creative, and aligned with the target audience.

Crafting Headlines

Effective headlines grab attention and entice the audience to learn more. Use prompts that specify tone, style, and purpose.

Prompt: "Generate three engaging headlines for a blog post about the

benefits of solar energy, focusing on environmental impact." AI Response:

"Powering the Planet: How Solar Energy is Saving Our Environment"
"From Sunlight to Sustainability: The Top Benefits of Solar Power"

"Clean Energy Revolution: Why Solar is the Future"

Writing Social Media Posts

Social media content should be concise, engaging, and tailored to the platform.

Prompt: "Write a Facebook post promoting a new eco-friendly water bottle, highlighting its sustainability and durability."

AI Response: "Stay hydrated and eco-conscious with our new reusable water bottle! Made from durable materials, it's perfect for every adventure while reducing plastic waste.   #EcoFriendly #StayHydrated"

Creating Ad Copy

Ads require persuasive language and a clear call to action (CTA).

Prompt: "Write a 30-word Google ad for a budget-friendly meal delivery service."

AI Response: "Delicious, healthy meals delivered to your doorstep for just $8.99! Save time and eat smart.

Try our meal delivery service today. Fresh, fast, and affordable. Order now!"

Using AI for Copywriting and Brand Messaging

AI can assist in developing cohesive brand messaging and copy that resonates with the audience.

Establishing a Brand Voice

Define the tone and style of communication for consistent messaging.

Prompt: "Describe the brand voice for a luxury skincare line targeting professional women in their 30s."

AI Response: "Sophisticated, empowering, and approachable. The tone should reflect elegance and expertise, emphasizing premium quality and self-care."

Writing Product Descriptions

Detailed, enticing product descriptions can boost sales by highlighting key features and benefits.

Prompt: "Write a product description for a smartwatch with health tracking features."

AI Response: "Stay connected and healthy with our state-of-the-art smartwatch. Track your heart rate, monitor sleep, and get real-time notifications. Sleek, durable, and perfect for your active lifestyle."

Prompt Frameworks for Market Research

AI can support market research by analyzing trends, customer feedback, and competitor strategies.

Analyzing Trends

Prompts can help uncover emerging trends in your industry.

Prompt: "Identify the top three trends in

sustainable fashion for 2024." AI Response:

Increased use of recycled fabrics.

Rise of rental and resale platforms.

Adoption of biodegradable packaging.

Understanding Customer Needs

AI can synthesize customer reviews and feedback to highlight common desires or pain points.

Prompt: "Summarize common themes in customer reviews for our latest fitness app."

AI Response: "Users love the app's easy interface and workout variety. However, many request integration with wearable devices and additional customization options."

Competitor Analysis

Compare your business with competitors to identify strengths and opportunities.

Prompt: "Analyze the strengths and weaknesses of

Competitor X's social media strategy." AI Response:

Strengths: Consistent posting schedule, engaging visuals.

Weaknesses: Lack of user interaction, limited content diversity.

Exercises for Marketing and Content Creation

Exercise 1: Headline Crafting

Choose a topic: "Promoting renewable energy."

Write a prompt: "Generate three headlines for a social media campaign on renewable energy."

Analyze the AI's responses for creativity and alignment with the topic.

Exercise 2: Writing Ad Copy

Identify a product: "An ergonomic office chair."

Write a prompt: "Create a 25-word Instagram ad for an ergonomic office chair."

Evaluate the AI's response for clarity, engagement, and effectiveness.

Exercise 3: Market Research
Define a research area: "Trends in plant-based diets."
Write a prompt: "Identify three emerging trends in plant-

based diets for 2024." Review the AI's findings for relevance

and actionable insights.

Conclusion

Prompts for marketing and content creation enable businesses to craft engaging materials, refine brand messaging, and conduct insightful market research. By leveraging AI-driven tools, you can enhance your marketing strategies and connect with your audience more effectively. In the next chapter, we'll explore how to use AI prompts for strategic decision-making, helping you optimize your business operations.

Chapter 12: Strategic Decision-Making

Prompts for SWOT Analysis and Competitive Insights

Strategic decision-making requires a clear understanding of your business's strengths, weaknesses, opportunities, and threats (SWOT). AI can assist in gathering insights, analyzing data, and presenting actionable strategies.

Conducting a SWOT Analysis

AI can help frame and explore SWOT factors through targeted prompts.

Prompt: "List the strengths, weaknesses, opportunities, and threats for a small e-commerce business specializing in handmade jewelry." AI Response:

Strengths: Unique designs, personalized customer service.

Weaknesses: Limited production capacity, reliance on a single sales channel.

Opportunities: Expansion to global markets, collaboration with influencers.

Threats: Competition from mass-market brands, rising material costs.

Gaining Competitive Insights

AI can synthesize competitor information and industry trends to guide your strategic decisions.

Prompt: "Compare the marketing strategies of Competitor A and Competitor B in the health and wellness industry."

AI Response:

Competitor A: Focuses on digital ads and influencer partnerships.

Competitor B: Leverages community events and loyalty programs.

Scenario Planning and Forecasting

Scenario planning involves envisioning potential future events and preparing for them. AI can assist by generating plausible scenarios and analyzing their impact.

Exploring Potential Scenarios

Prompt: "Generate three scenarios for a retail business responding to economic downturns." AI Response:

Conservative: Reduce inventory and focus on essential products.

Moderate: Launch discounts to boost sales and retain customers.

Aggressive: Invest in online sales channels to offset declining in-store traffic.

Forecasting Trends

Prompt: "Forecast the impact of remote work trends on the co-working space industry in the next five years." AI Response:

Increased demand for hybrid office models.

Growth in smaller, regional co-working hubs.

Emphasis on flexibility and subscription-based pricing.

Enhancing Team Collaboration Through AI

AI can improve team collaboration by facilitating communication, streamlining workflows, and providing decision support.

Facilitating Effective Meetings

AI can assist in planning and managing productive meetings.
Prompt: "Draft an agenda for a team meeting focused on improving customer retention." AI Response:

- Review current retention metrics.
- Discuss customer feedback trends.
- Brainstorm retention strategies.
- Assign action items and deadlines.
- Streamlining Workflow Processes

AI can suggest tools and methods to enhance team productivity.
Prompt: "What tools can help a remote marketing team collaborate effectively?" AI Response:

Trello for project management.

Slack for real-time communication.

Canva for collaborative design projects.

Supporting Data-Driven Decisions

AI can analyze data and present actionable insights to guide team decisions.
Prompt: "Analyze sales data from the past year and suggest strategies to improve Q1 performance." AI Response:

Focus on top-performing products and replicate successful campaigns.

Address declining sales in underperforming regions with targeted promotions.

Exercises for Strategic Decision-Making

Exercise 1: SWOT Analysis
Choose a business: "A local coffee shop."
Write a prompt: "List the strengths, weaknesses, opportunities, and threats for a local coffee shop."
Evaluate the AI's analysis and identify areas for strategic improvement.

Exercise 2: Scenario Planning
Define a challenge: "Adapting to increasing e-commerce competition."
Write a prompt: "Generate three scenarios for a brick-and-mortar store

adapting to e-commerce competition." Discuss the feasibility of each

scenario.

Exercise 3: Enhancing Team Collaboration
Identify a collaboration challenge: "Improving cross-department communication."
Write a prompt: "Suggest strategies and tools to improve cross-department communication in a mid-sized company."

Implement one suggestion and assess its impact.

Conclusion

AI-driven prompts for strategic decision-making provide valuable insights for SWOT analysis, scenario planning, and enhancing team collaboration. By leveraging these tools, businesses can make informed, datadriven decisions and adapt to changing environments effectively. In the next chapter, we'll explore how to use AI prompts for web design, optimizing both creativity and functionality.

Chapter 13: Prompt Engineering for Web Design
Crafting Prompts for Layout and Design Generation

Web design requires a balance between aesthetics and functionality. AI can assist by generating layouts, suggesting design elements, and providing inspiration for various web design tasks.

Generating Layout Ideas

Prompts can guide AI to create layout options tailored to specific industries or purposes.

Prompt: "Suggest a minimalist website layout for a boutique coffee shop." AI Response:

Header: Large, high-quality image of a coffee cup with the shop's logo.

Navigation Bar: Sticky bar with links to Menu, About Us, Locations, and Contact.

Main Content: Highlight daily specials and customer testimonials.

Footer: Social media icons, newsletter sign-up, and contact information.

Selecting Design Elements

AI can recommend color schemes, fonts, and images that align with a brand's identity.

Prompt: "Suggest a color palette and typography for a modern tech startup's website." AI Response:

Color Palette: Shades of blue and gray with accents of orange.

Typography: Sans-serif fonts like Roboto or Open Sans for a clean and professional look.

Creating Interactive Features

Prompts can help ideate interactive elements that enhance user engagement.

Prompt: "What interactive features can be included in a travel agency's website?" AI Response:

Destination map with clickable hotspots.

Trip planner tool with customizable itineraries.

Chatbot for instant travel advice.

Using AI Tools for Wire framing and Prototyping

Wire framing and prototyping are essential steps in web design. AI can streamline these processes by generating initial frameworks and interactive prototypes.

Wireframe Creation

Prompt: "Create a wireframe layout for a non-profit organization's homepage." AI Response:

Header: Logo, mission statement, and navigation bar.

Main Section: Hero image with a donation call-to-action.

Subsections: Highlight ongoing projects, volunteer testimonials, and upcoming events.

Footer: Links to social media, newsletter subscription, and contact form.

Interactive Prototyping
AI tools can generate prototypes with clickable elements to test user flows.
Prompt: "Design an interactive prototype for an e-commerce website's product page." AI Response:

Product images with zoom and 360-degree view options.

Add-to-cart button with dynamic quantity selector.

Customer reviews section with filters for ratings.

Streamlining Workflows for Content-Heavy Sites
Content-heavy websites, such as blogs or news portals, require efficient organization and searchability. AI can optimize these workflows by structuring content and suggesting user-friendly layouts.

Organizing Content

Prompt: "How should articles be categorized on a tech blog to improve user navigation?" AI Response:

Divide articles into categories like Gadgets, Software, Reviews, and Industry News.

Use tags for specific topics such as AI, Blockchain, and Cloud Computing.

Add a search bar with filters for date and popularity.

Enhancing User Experience

Prompt: "Suggest features to improve the

readability of a news portal." AI Response:

Implement a dark mode toggle for night readers.

Add font size adjustment options.

Include summaries or key points at the start of articles.

Practical Examples and Templates for Web Design

AI-generated templates can provide a starting point for web design projects, saving time and ensuring consistency.

Examples of Prompts

E-commerce Website:

Prompt: "Design a homepage layout for

an online bookstore." AI Response:

Hero banner showcasing bestsellers.

Category carousel for genres like Fiction, Non-Fiction, and Children's Books.

Newsletter subscription form at the bottom.

Portfolio Website:

Prompt: "Suggest a layout for a

photographer's portfolio site." AI Response:

Full-screen carousel of featured images.

Grid gallery with clickable thumbnails.
Contact form with links to social media.

Educational Website:

Prompt: "Create a template for an

online learning platform." AI Response:

Course catalog with search and filter options.

Dashboard for tracking progress.

Discussion forums for peer interaction.

Exercises for Web Design Prompt Engineering

Exercise 1: Layout Generation

Identify a type of website: "A fitness blog."

Write a prompt: "Design a homepage layout for a fitness blog targeting beginners."

Analyze the AI's response and refine the layout.

Exercise 2: Interactive Features

Define a website goal: "Increase engagement on a travel website."

Write a prompt: "Suggest three interactive features to increase

engagement on a travel website." Evaluate and implement the

suggestions.

Exercise 3: Prototyping

Choose a website section: "Product page for an e-commerce store."

Write a prompt: "Create an interactive prototype for an e-commerce product page focusing on user convenience."

Test the prototype with user feedback.

Conclusion

AI-driven prompt engineering can revolutionize web design by providing layout ideas, wireframes, and interactive prototypes tailored to specific needs. By using structured prompts, designers can save time, enhance creativity, and improve user experiences. In the next chapter, we'll explore how AI prompts can elevate graphic design projects, including branding and visual storytelling.

Chapter 14: Prompt Engineering for Graphic Design

Designing Prompts for Illustrations, Logos, and Branding

AI tools can assist in generating ideas for illustrations, logos, and branding that align with a specific vision or target audience. By crafting precise prompts, you can guide the AI toward creative and relevant outputs.

Creating Illustrations

Illustrations can enhance visual storytelling in various mediums. AI tools can suggest concepts or even generate drafts based on your requirements.

Prompt: "Design an illustration of a futuristic city with

green energy solutions." AI Response:

High-rise buildings with vertical gardens.

Solar panels and wind turbines integrated into the landscape.

Hovering vehicles powered by renewable energy.

Developing Logos

A logo represents a brand's identity and must convey its values effectively. Prompts for logo design should specify the brand's industry, audience, and core message.

Prompt: "Create a modern logo for a vegan

restaurant targeting millennials." AI Response:

A clean, minimalist design featuring a leafy green V.

Earth-tone color palette to emphasize sustainability.

Rounded fonts to create an approachable feel.

Building Branding Concepts

Branding encompasses visual elements and tone, which can be refined using AI prompts.

Prompt: "Suggest a branding concept for a luxury skincare line

emphasizing natural ingredients." AI Response:

Visuals: Soft pastel colors, botanical illustrations.

Typography: Elegant serif fonts for a premium feel.

Tone: Sophisticated, nurturing, and eco-conscious.

Leveraging AI for Color Schemes, Typography, and Composition

AI can assist in creating harmonious color schemes, selecting appropriate fonts, and composing balanced designs that resonate with the target audience.

Generating Color Schemes

Prompts can guide AI to develop palettes based on themes or emotions.

Prompt: "Create a vibrant color palette for a

children's educational app." AI Response:

Primary colors: Bright yellow, blue, and red for energy.

Accent colors: Lime green and orange for warmth and fun.

Choosing Typography

Fonts convey mood and readability, which are critical in graphic design.

Prompt: "Suggest fonts for a tech company's website

aiming for a futuristic feel." AI Response:

Headline Font: Roboto or Exo for a modern aesthetic.

Body Font: Open Sans for readability.

Refining Composition

Composition ensures that design elements are visually appealing and functional.

Prompt: "How should elements be arranged on a poster

advertising a music festival?" AI Response:

Center the festival's name at the top in bold typography.

Place featured artist names below the header.

Add event details at the bottom with icons for time and location.

Iterative Refinement in Visual Projects

Iteration is key to refining graphic designs. AI can provide alternative suggestions or adapt to feedback.

Generating Variations

Prompt: "Create three variations of a logo for a

fitness app named 'Pulse.'" AI Response:

A heartbeat icon integrated with the letter P.

A circular logo representing motion and vitality.

A minimalist logo using bold typography and subtle waveforms.

Adapting to Feedback

Feedback: "The logo looks too busy. Simplify the design and emphasize the heartbeat icon."

AI Refinement: "Simplified the logo by removing waveforms and enlarging the heartbeat icon for clarity."

Tips for Blending Human Creativity with AI Support

While AI can expedite graphic design tasks, human input ensures originality and emotional resonance. Effective collaboration involves:

Clear Communication: Define goals and preferences explicitly in prompts.

Critical Evaluation: Assess AI-generated outputs critically, refining them as needed.

Experimentation: Use AI to explore unconventional ideas, then adapt them to fit the project's vision.

Exercises for Graphic Design Prompts

Exercise 1: Creating Logos
Identify a business: "An online bookstore."

Write a prompt: "Design a logo for an online bookstore targeting young adults, emphasizing creativity and knowledge."
Analyze the AI's designs and select the most fitting concept.

Exercise 2: Generating Color Schemes
Define a theme: "Eco-friendly products."
Write a prompt: "Create a color palette for a brand selling eco-

friendly cleaning supplies." Test the palette for harmony and

alignment with the brand message.

Exercise 3: Refining Compositions
State a design need: "Flyer for a charity run."

Write a prompt: "Suggest a balanced composition for a flyer promoting a charity run, including space for images and text."

Evaluate the composition and refine it iteratively.

Conclusion

Prompt engineering for graphic design empowers creatives to produce compelling visuals efficiently while maintaining artistic integrity. By leveraging AI for illustrations, branding, and iterative refinement, designers can elevate their work. In the next chapter, we'll explore advanced techniques for mastering prompt templates, enhancing consistency and productivity in design projects.

Chapter 15: Mastering Prompt Templates

Reusable Structures for Common Tasks

Prompt templates are structured formats designed for consistency and efficiency in interacting with AI. These templates can be adapted for various scenarios, saving time and ensuring quality outputs.

What Are Prompt Templates?

Prompt templates provide a reusable framework for creating effective prompts. By standardizing the structure, users can focus on the specific content or task while ensuring clarity and precision.

Benefits of Using Templates

Consistency: Maintain a uniform approach across similar tasks.

Efficiency: Reduce the time spent crafting new prompts from scratch.

Scalability: Easily adapt templates for different applications.

Example of a Template for

Summaries Template:

"Summarize [topic/document] by highlighting the main points, [specify format, e.g., bullet points or paragraphs], and provide [additional context or emphasis]." Example:

"Summarize the article on climate change by highlighting the main points in bullet points and emphasize the economic implications."

Creating Templates for Life and Business Scenarios

Templates can be tailored for personal and professional tasks, ensuring adaptability and relevance.

Personal Productivity

Task: Planning daily activities.

Template:

"Create a schedule for [day/week] that includes time for [specific tasks], with a focus on [prioritization, breaks, etc.]."

Example:

"Create a schedule for Monday that includes time for work, exercise, and family, prioritizing morning productivity."

Professional Tasks

Task: Writing professional emails.

Template:

"Draft an email to [recipient] about [topic], ensuring it is [tone: formal/informal], and includes [specific details or attachments]." Example:

"Draft an email to the marketing team about the upcoming product launch, ensuring it is formal and includes the launch timeline."

Creative Projects

Task: Brainstorming ideas.

Template:

"Generate [number] ideas for [specific goal or project], focusing on [theme or constraints]." Example:

"Generate 10 ideas for a social media campaign promoting eco-friendly products, focusing on engaging visuals."

Sharing and Collaborating with Templates

Templates are not only personal tools but also valuable resources for teams. Sharing standardized templates ensures everyone follows best practices and produces consistent results.

Creating a Template Library

Categorize Templates: Group templates by task or purpose, such as marketing, project management, or learning.

Document Examples: Include sample prompts and expected outputs for clarity.

Regular Updates: Adapt templates based on feedback and changing needs.

Collaborative Usage

Scenario: Team brainstorming sessions.

Template:
"Collaborate to generate [number] solutions for [problem], considering [specific criteria]." Example:

"Collaborate to generate 5 solutions for reducing delivery times, considering cost efficiency and customer satisfaction."

Exercises for Mastering Templates

Exercise 1: Designing a Template
Identify a recurring task: "Preparing

meeting agendas." Create a template:

"Draft a meeting agenda for [meeting purpose], including [key topics,

time allocation, and participants]." Test the template with different

scenarios.

Exercise 2: Adapting Templates
Start with a general template: "Write a product description for [item], highlighting [features and benefits]."

Adapt it for specific needs: "Write a product description for a smartwatch, highlighting health tracking and connectivity features."

Compare outputs to assess adaptability.

Exercise 3: Sharing Templates
Choose a team task: "Generating

project updates." Create a shared

template:

"Summarize project updates for [team/project], focusing on

[milestones, challenges, and next steps]." Gather feedback from the team

to refine the template.

Conclusion

Mastering prompt templates empowers individuals and teams to work more efficiently and consistently. By creating, sharing, and iterating on templates, you can streamline workflows and enhance collaboration. In the next chapter, we will delve into leveraging AI creativity for artistic, literary, and innovative projects, expanding the possibilities of prompt engineering.

Chapter 16: Leveraging AI Creativity

Experimenting with Abstract and Divergent Prompts

AI tools excel at generating creative and unexpected ideas when guided by abstract or divergent prompts. These prompts encourage the AI to think beyond conventional patterns and explore imaginative possibilities.

Encouraging Abstract Thinking

Abstract prompts allow AI to generate ideas that are not bound by strict rules or expectations.

Prompt: "Describe a utopian city in the year 3000, focusing on technology and nature integration." AI Response:

A city powered entirely by renewable energy, with transparent solar panels on skyscrapers.

Floating gardens irrigated by recycled water.

AI systems managing resource distribution to eliminate waste.

Generating Divergent Ideas

Divergent prompts inspire multiple solutions or interpretations.
Prompt: "List 10 unconventional uses for a smartphone in an emergency." AI Response:

Emergency flashlight using the screen.

Distress signal through flashing lights.

Improvised magnifying glass using the camera lens.

Sound amplifier with a makeshift cone, and more.

Using AI for Artistic, Literary, and Design Projects

AI can serve as a creative collaborator in artistic endeavors, from visual art to storytelling and music composition.

Visual Art

Prompts can guide AI to generate visual concepts or refine artistic ideas.
Prompt: "Create a concept for a surreal painting featuring a clock and an ocean." AI Response:

A clock melting into the waves of an ocean under a crimson sky.

Hands of the clock forming bridges to distant islands.

Literary Projects

AI can assist in writing poems, short stories, or entire chapters.

Prompt: "Write a poem about the change of seasons in

the style of Robert Frost." AI Response:

"The autumn leaves fall soft and slow, / A whispered chill in winds that blow..."

Music and Sound

AI tools can suggest compositions or lyrics based on themes or emotions.

Prompt: "Compose lyrics for a song about hope and resilience."

AI Response:

Verse: "Through the storm, the light will shine, / Every shadow fades in time..."

Balancing Human Intuition with AI Capabilities

While AI provides inspiration and efficiency, human intuition ensures emotional depth and alignment with creative goals.

Integrating AI Suggestions

Evaluate Outputs: Assess AI-generated ideas critically, refining them to match the vision.

Add Personal Touch: Incorporate unique elements or styles to differentiate the final product.

Avoiding Over-Reliance

Use AI as a Springboard: Treat AI suggestions as starting points, not final answers.

Maintain Authenticity: Balance AI's efficiency with human creativity to preserve originality.

Exercises for Exploring AI Creativity

Exercise 1: Abstract Prompts

Write an abstract prompt: "Imagine a world where gravity works in reverse."

Analyze the AI's response for creativity and feasibility.

Refine the prompt to focus on specific aspects, such as architecture or daily life.

Exercise 2: Collaborative Storytelling
Start a story: "In a quiet village, a mysterious light appeared in the sky one night..."
Use a prompt to continue: "Write the next two paragraphs, focusing on the villagers' reaction." Evaluate the AI's contribution and adapt it to fit the narrative.

Exercise 3: Creative Design
Define a project: "Logo for a futuristic space tourism company."
Write a prompt: "Suggest three logo concepts for a company offering luxury space travel." Assess the concepts for originality and alignment with the brand's image.

Conclusion

Leveraging AI for creativity opens new avenues for artistic and innovative projects. By experimenting with abstract prompts and combining AI capabilities with human intuition, creators can produce unique and impactful work. In the next chapter, we'll explore ethical considerations and responsible use of AI in creative and professional contexts.

Chapter 17: Ethics and Responsible Use

Avoiding Biases in Prompts

AI systems are trained on vast datasets that may contain biases. Prompt engineering can either mitigate or exacerbate these biases, depending on how prompts are crafted.

Understanding AI Bias

Biases in AI arise from:

Training Data: If the data contains stereotypes or imbalances, the model may reproduce them.

Prompt Design: Poorly constructed prompts can unintentionally reinforce biased assumptions.

Strategies to Avoid Bias

Use Neutral Language:

Problematic Prompt: "Why are men better at leadership roles?"

Neutral Prompt: "What are the qualities of effective leadership across genders?"

Specify Context:

Avoid vague prompts that might lead to biased outputs.

Example: Instead of "Who are the greatest scientists?" specify, "Who are notable scientists in physics from diverse backgrounds?"

Test and Refine:

Generate multiple outputs and review them for unintended biases.

Adjust the prompt to guide the AI toward balanced perspectives.

Ensuring Privacy and Data Security in AI Interactions

AI systems often process sensitive information. Ethical use of AI requires safeguarding user privacy and securing data.

Principles of Data Privacy

Minimize Data Collection:

Only input the information necessary for the task.

Example: Avoid including personal identifiers in prompts unless essential.

Avoid Sharing Sensitive Information:

Refrain from providing proprietary or personal data that could be stored or misused.

Example: Use placeholders for confidential details, like "[Client Name]" or "[Project Code]."

Understand Data Usage Policies:

Familiarize yourself with the AI platform's data handling practices.

Ensure compliance with relevant regulations like GDPR or CCPA.

Ethical Considerations in Business Applications

AI can streamline business operations, but its use must align with ethical standards to maintain trust and integrity.

Transparent Communication

Disclose AI Use:

Inform users when they are interacting with an AI system.

Example: Add a disclaimer like, "This response was generated by an AI assistant."

Explain Limitations:

Be upfront about the AI's capabilities and constraints.
Example: "This tool provides suggestions but does not

replace professional advice." Fair Decision-Making

Avoid Discriminatory Practices:

Use prompts that ensure fairness in hiring, lending, or other decisions.

Example: "List candidates based on qualifications and experience, disregarding personal attributes like age or gender."

Regular Audits:

Periodically review AI outputs for biases or errors.

Incorporate diverse perspectives in evaluation processes.

Promoting Ethical AI Use in Creative Fields

AI's ability to generate content raises questions about authorship,

originality, and fair usage. Respecting Intellectual Property

Avoid Plagiarism:

Ensure AI-generated content does not replicate existing works without proper attribution.

Example: Verify outputs against plagiarism detection tools.

Attribute Collaborative Contributions:

Acknowledge AI's role in creative projects where appropriate.
Example: "This design concept was developed using AI tools."

Encouraging Transparency

Identify AI-Generated Content:

Clearly label AI-created works to differentiate them from human creations.

Example: "This illustration was created with the assistance of AI software."

Avoid Deceptive Practices:

Do not use AI outputs to impersonate individuals or spread misinformation.

Example: Craft prompts that prioritize factual and ethical communication.

Exercises for Ethical and Responsible AI Use

Exercise 1: Identifying Biases

Write a prompt: "List the greatest leaders in history."

Analyze the AI's response for diversity and representation.

Refine the prompt: "List influential leaders from different

cultures and time periods." Exercise 2: Ensuring Data Privacy

Create a scenario: "Draft an email summarizing client feedback."

Write a prompt: "Summarize client feedback without including identifying information."

Verify the AI's response for privacy compliance.

Exercise 3: Ethical Business Applications

Define a task: "Screen resumes for a software developer position."

Write a prompt: "Evaluate candidates based on technical skills and relevant experience, excluding personal details."

Assess the output for fairness and inclusivity.

Conclusion

Ethical and responsible use of AI ensures that its benefits are maximized while minimizing potential harms. By addressing biases, safeguarding privacy, and adhering to ethical standards, users can build trust and integrity into AI-driven interactions. In the next chapter, we will explore how to establish a prompting workflow to ensure repeatable success and continuous improvement.

Chapter 18: Establishing a Prompting Workflow

Designing Systems for Repeatable Success

A well-structured prompting workflow ensures consistent and effective AI interactions. By standardizing processes, users can achieve reliable results and continually improve outcomes.

Key Elements of a Prompting Workflow

Define Objectives:

Clearly outline what you want to achieve with the AI.

Example: "Generate a summary of weekly sales reports focusing on trends and anomalies."

Choose the Right Prompt Structure:

Select a format that aligns with the task, such as open-ended, closed-ended, or multi-step prompts.

Example: "List the top-performing products this week and

explain their success factors." Test and Refine Prompts:

Start with a draft prompt and evaluate the AI's response.

Adjust for clarity, specificity, and alignment with objectives.

Standardize Templates:

Create reusable templates for recurring tasks to save time and ensure consistency.

Example Template: "Summarize [data/topic] in [format], focusing on [specific criteria]."

Tracking and Measuring Effectiveness of Prompts

To improve your workflow, it's essential to track the performance of your prompts and measure their effectiveness.

Metrics for Evaluating Prompts

Relevance:

Does the AI's response align with the prompt's objectives?

Assessment: Compare the response to your expected outcome.

Clarity:

Is the response easy to understand and free from ambiguity?

Improvement Tip: Simplify language or add context if needed.

Completeness:

Does the response address all parts of the prompt?

Improvement Tip: Specify all required elements in the prompt.

Efficiency:

How quickly can the prompt produce usable results?

Improvement Tip: Refine prompts to minimize back-and-forth iterations.

Tools for Monitoring Performance

Feedback Systems:

Use feedback loops to refine prompts based on user or team input. Example: "Was this response helpful? Yes/No. Provide suggestions

for improvement." Version Control:

Maintain a record of prompt iterations to track changes and their impact.
Example: Label prompts with version numbers (e.g., "Prompt v1.0").

Continuous Improvement Through Feedback Loops

Feedback is a critical component of an effective prompting workflow. It allows for iterative refinement and ensures that prompts evolve with changing needs.

Sources of Feedback

User Input:

Gather insights from those who interact with the AI system.
Example: "Does this summary meet your expectations? What could be improved?"

AI Performance Analysis:

Evaluate the quality and consistency of AI-generated responses.

Example: Analyze responses for recurring errors or gaps.

Scenario Testing:

Test prompts across different use cases to ensure versatility.

Example: Use the same prompt for summarizing different types of reports.

Refining Prompts Based on Feedback

Identify Issues:

Determine specific areas where the prompt failed to deliver.

Example: "The response didn't include key sales metrics."

Implement Adjustments:

Modify the prompt to address identified gaps.

Example: Add, "Include metrics such as revenue, units sold, and customer retention rates."

Re-Test and Re-Evaluate:

Apply the revised prompt and measure its effectiveness.

Repeat until optimal results are achieved.

Exercises for Building a Prompting Workflow

Exercise 1: Creating a Workflow

Define a task: "Summarize customer feedback from the past month." Design a workflow:

Draft an initial prompt.

Test the prompt with sample feedback data.
Refine based on the AI's response.

Standardize the process for future use.
Exercise 2: Evaluating Prompt Effectiveness
Write a prompt: "Generate a report on employee productivity metrics." Use metrics to evaluate:

Relevance: Does it cover key productivity indicators?

Completeness: Are any important metrics missing?

Modify the prompt as needed.

Exercise 3: Implementing Feedback Loops
Collect feedback on a prompt's output: "Draft an email campaign for a new product launch."
Ask for user feedback: "Does this draft align with the brand's tone and objectives?" Adjust the prompt and re-test.

Conclusion

Establishing a robust prompting workflow ensures consistency, efficiency, and continuous improvement in AI interactions. By defining objectives, tracking performance, and incorporating feedback loops, you can optimize your use of AI tools. In the next chapter, we will explore real-world case studies and applications, demonstrating how these workflows can be applied across different industries.

Chapter 19: Case Studies and Real-World Applications

Examples from Life, Education, and Business

AI-powered prompting can solve problems, streamline processes, and spark innovation across various domains. Real-world case studies illustrate the practical applications and benefits of prompt engineering.

Life: Personal Productivity

Scenario

Challenge: Managing a busy schedule with conflicting priorities.

Solution:

Prompt: "Create a daily schedule for a working parent with meetings, a child's soccer practice, and meal prep."

AI Output:

Morning: 7:00-8:00 AM – Prepare breakfast and pack lunches.

Midday: 12:00-1:00 PM – Virtual meeting.

Evening: 6:00-7:30 PM – Soccer practice.

Late Evening: 8:00-8:30 PM – Plan meals for the next day.

Outcome

Efficient time management reduced stress and improved daily productivity.

Education: Enhancing Learning Outcomes

Scenario

Challenge: Helping high school students understand complex concepts in biology.

Solution:
Prompt: "Explain the process of photosynthesis in simple

terms for high school students." AI Output:

"Photosynthesis is how plants make their food. They use sunlight, water,

and carbon dioxide to produce oxygen and glucose, which gives them energy."

Outcome

Students grasped the concept more quickly, leading to better engagement and retention.

Business: Customer Interaction

Scenario

Challenge: Reducing response times for frequently asked questions in an online store.

Solution:
Prompt: "Provide a clear response to the question:

'What is your return policy?'" AI Output:

"Our return policy allows returns within 30 days of purchase with the original receipt. Items must be unused and in their original packaging."

Outcome

Automated responses reduced average customer query resolution time by 40%.

Lessons Learned from Successful Prompt Strategies

Tailoring Prompts to the Audience

Example: Simplifying technical explanations for non-experts increases comprehension.

Key Takeaway: Understand the user's knowledge level and adjust prompts accordingly.

Iterative Refinement

Example: Refining a marketing prompt from "Create an ad for a new product" to "Write a Facebook ad targeting young adults for our eco-friendly water bottles."

Key Takeaway: Precision in prompts leads to more actionable and relevant outputs.

Encouraging Creativity

Example: Prompting AI to "Suggest three innovative

uses for recycled plastic." Key Takeaway: Open-ended

prompts can unlock innovative solutions.

Adapting Prompts for Different Industries

Healthcare

Prompt: "Summarize patient feedback on recent clinic visits, focusing on suggestions for improvement." Application: Streamlining quality improvement initiatives.

Finance

Prompt: "Analyze quarterly sales data and identify trends."

Application: Enhancing decision-making for investment strategies.

Retail

Prompt: "Generate ideas for a summer marketing campaign for a clothing store." Application: Increasing seasonal sales through targeted promotions.

Technology

Prompt: "Explain blockchain technology to a non-technical audience." Application: Educating clients on complex innovations.

Exercises for Real-World Applications

Exercise 1: Personal Productivity
Identify a task: "Planning a weekend itinerary."

Write a prompt: "Create a two-day itinerary for a family trip to a national park, including activities for all ages."
Evaluate the AI's response for feasibility and variety.

Exercise 2: Education
Define a concept: "Explaining gravity to middle school students."
Write a prompt: "Explain gravity in simple terms, using examples from everyday life." Assess the clarity and engagement of the response.

Exercise 3: Business

State a need: "Improving customer engagement on social media."
Write a prompt: "Suggest five social media post ideas to

promote a new fitness app." Test the effectiveness of the AI's

suggestions.

Conclusion
Case studies demonstrate how AI-driven prompts can address challenges and unlock opportunities across various domains. By analyzing successes and lessons learned, users can adapt these strategies to fit their unique needs. In the next chapter, we will explore scaling and automation, focusing on how to integrate prompts into larger workflows for organizational efficiency. Chapter 20: Scaling and Automation

Automating Repetitive Tasks with Prompt Libraries
Scaling AI interactions often involves automating repetitive tasks. Prompt libraries—collections of reusable prompts—streamline workflows and maintain consistency across large-scale operations.

What Are Prompt Libraries?
Prompt libraries are centralized repositories of pre-designed prompts tailored to specific tasks. These libraries:

Save time by eliminating the need to recreate prompts.

Ensure uniformity in outputs across teams or projects.

Provide templates for rapid deployment in diverse scenarios.

Building a Prompt Library
Identify Common Tasks:

Examples: Summarizing reports, drafting emails, generating social media posts.

Create Modular Prompts:
Design prompts that are adaptable with placeholders for variables.
Example: "Summarize [type of document] in [format], highlighting [key focus areas]."

Organize by Category:
Group prompts by use case, such as marketing, analytics, or customer support.

Test and Refine:
Validate the prompts for accuracy and adaptability across scenarios.

Integrating Prompts into Organizational Processes

Embedding prompt engineering into organizational workflows enhances efficiency and scalability.

Incorporating AI in Team Workflows

Standardizing Tasks:

Use predefined prompts for repetitive tasks like report generation or customer queries.

Example: "Generate a weekly performance summary

for the sales team." Enhancing Collaboration:

Shared access to prompt libraries ensures consistency across teams.

Example: "Draft a project update email for all stakeholders,

summarizing milestones and next steps." Scaling Across Departments

Marketing:

Automate content creation for blogs, ads, and social media.

Example: "Write three engaging LinkedIn posts about our

new product launch." Operations:

Streamline logistics with AI-assisted scheduling and planning.

Example: "Create a delivery schedule for the week,

prioritizing high-demand areas." HR:

Simplify hiring and onboarding processes with automated templates.
Example: "Draft a job posting for a software developer role, emphasizing remote work opportunities."

Tools and Platforms for Scalable Prompt Engineering

AI platforms and tools enable organizations to implement scalable prompt engineering systems effectively.

Popular Tools

OpenAI API:

Offers customization options for integrating prompts into existing workflows.

Zapier and Automation Tools:

Connects AI platforms with other software for seamless automation.

Example: Use Zapier to trigger AI-generated responses for incoming customer queries.

AI-Powered Project Management Tools:

Platforms like Monday.com or Asana with AI integrations streamline task allocation and tracking.

Setting Up Automation Pipelines
Define Triggers:

Identify events that activate AI-generated responses.

Example: Customer inquiry triggers a chatbot response.

Map Workflows:

Outline the sequence of tasks and prompts.
Example: Inquiry → Categorization → Response generation → Escalation if needed.

Test and Optimize:

Monitor the pipeline for bottlenecks and refine as necessary.

Exercises for Scaling and Automation
Exercise 1: Building a Prompt Library
Identify repetitive tasks in your workflow: "Daily performance summaries."
Create a modular prompt: "Summarize daily performance

metrics, including [specific indicators]." Test the prompt with sample

data and refine it. Exercise 2: Automating a Workflow

Define a workflow: "Customer support

query resolution." Write a sequence of

prompts:

Step 1: "Categorize the customer query by topic."
Step 2: "Generate a response for common issues in [category]."

Step 3: "Escalate to a human agent if unresolved in

two interactions." Implement and test the workflow.

Exercise 3: Integrating Tools
Choose a tool: "Zapier."

Create an automation pipeline:
Trigger: "New customer inquiry received."
Action: "Use AI to draft a response."

Evaluate the effectiveness of the integration.

Conclusion

Scaling and automation through prompt libraries and AI tools enable organizations to optimize efficiency and maintain consistency across large operations. By integrating these techniques into workflows, teams can focus on strategic tasks while leveraging AI for repetitive processes. In the next chapter, we will explore creating personalized prompt portfolios to showcase expertise and enable further professional development.

Chapter 20: Creating Your Prompt Portfolio

Developing a Library of Personalized Prompts

A prompt portfolio is a curated collection of prompts tailored to your needs, showcasing your expertise in leveraging AI tools for various applications. It serves as both a resource and a demonstration of your proficiency.

Why Create a Prompt Portfolio?

Showcase Expertise:

Demonstrates your ability to craft effective prompts.

Highlights versatility across domains like marketing, education, or problem-solving.

Streamline Workflows:

Provides ready-to-use prompts for common tasks.

Reduces the time spent on crafting new prompts.

Enable Collaboration:

Serves as a resource for teams or clients to understand and replicate your strategies.

Steps to Build Your Portfolio

Identify Key Areas:

- Focus on domains relevant to your personal or professional goals.
- Examples: Customer support, creative writing, strategic planning.

Organize by Categories:

- Group prompts into categories like task management, brainstorming, or analysis.
- Use headings and subcategories for easy navigation.

Document Outcomes:

- Include examples of AI responses to illustrate the effectiveness of each prompt.

Refine Over Time:

- Update prompts based on feedback or new applications.

Showcasing Expertise Through Prompt-Based Projects

Your prompt portfolio can serve as a showcase of real-world applications, highlighting the impact of your AI interactions.

Example Projects

Marketing Campaigns:
Prompt: "Generate three social media posts promoting

eco-friendly products." Outcome: Increased engagement by

30% on Instagram posts.

Educational Tools:
Prompt: "Explain the concept of gravity in simple terms for

middle school students." Outcome: Improved student

comprehension based on feedback.

Business Analysis:

Prompt: "Analyze quarterly sales data and suggest strategies to boost performance in underperforming regions."
Outcome: Identified actionable insights that increased regional sales by 15%.

Formatting Your Portfolio

Introduction:

Brief overview of your expertise and goals for the portfolio.

Sections:

Organized by category with clear examples.

Visuals:

Include screenshots or charts to demonstrate AI-generated outputs.

Sharing and Monetizing Your Knowledge

Your prompt portfolio can be shared as a resource or turned into a monetizable asset.

Sharing for Collaboration

Teams:

Provide access to your portfolio to improve consistency in team outputs.

Clients:

Share tailored prompt libraries to enhance client deliverables.

Online Platforms:

Publish your portfolio on professional networks or as part of your personal website.

Monetizing Your Portfolio

Courses and Workshops:

Use your portfolio as the foundation for teaching prompt engineering.

Offer hands-on activities where participants adapt your prompts to their needs.

Consulting Services:

Develop custom prompt libraries for businesses or organizations.

Provide training sessions to improve their AI interactions.

E-Books or Templates:

Compile your prompts into a downloadable resource.

Sell specialized templates for niche applications, like content creation or analytics.

Exercises for Building and Using a Prompt Portfolio

Exercise 1: Categorizing Prompts
List 10 prompts you've created.

Organize them into categories like creative, analytical, or operational.

Review for gaps or overlaps and refine

accordingly. Exercise 2: Documenting

Outcomes

Select a prompt: "Create a content

calendar for a tech blog." Use it with AI to

generate a response.

Record the results and any improvements made during the process.

Exercise 3: Sharing and Feedback

Share a section of your portfolio with a peer or team.

Request feedback on clarity, relevance, and usability.

Revise the portfolio based on their input.

Conclusion

Creating a prompt portfolio empowers you to demonstrate your skills, streamline workflows, and even generate income through consulting or teaching. By organizing and refining your prompts, you establish a resource that evolves with your expertise. In the next chapter, we will explore turning this knowledge into a structured online course, extending its reach and impact.

Chapter 21: Building an Online Course

Structuring Course Content from the Book

Transforming your knowledge into an online course involves breaking down concepts into digestible modules and aligning them with clear learning objectives. This structured approach ensures participants gain actionable skills and insights. Steps to Structure Your Course Define Your Audience:

Identify their background, goals, and knowledge level.
Example: "Adults with minimal AI experience looking to improve

productivity and creativity." Outline Learning Objectives:

Specify what participants should achieve by the end of the course.

Example: "By the end of this course, participants will create effective AI prompts for personal productivity and business applications."

Divide Content into Modules:

Group related topics into cohesive sections.

Example Modules:

Introduction to Prompt Engineering.

Building Effective Prompts.

Applying Prompts to Personal and Professional Scenarios.

Advanced Techniques and Ethical Considerations.

Include Real-World Examples:

Demonstrate concepts with practical case studies and AI outputs.

Example: Show how a well-crafted prompt improved customer support efficiency.

Create a Logical Flow:

Arrange modules in a sequence that builds progressively on skills.

Example:

Start with foundational concepts.

Progress to intermediate and advanced applications.

Creating Engaging Activities and Assignments
Interactive activities and assignments keep participants engaged and encourage practical application of learned concepts.

Designing Activities

Scenario-Based Exercises:

Present real-world scenarios requiring prompt creation or refinement. Example: "Write a prompt to generate a marketing campaign

for a local bakery." Collaborative Projects:

Encourage group work to simulate team-based problem-solving. Example: "As a team, create a prompt library for a

customer service chatbot." Iterative Refinement Tasks:

Assign participants to improve prompts and compare results.

Example: Provide a vague prompt and have participants

refine it for clarity and specificity. Structuring Assignments

Objective:

Clearly define the goal of the assignment. Example: "Develop three prompts for generating blog post ideas

targeting small business owners." Instructions:

Provide step-by-step guidance to complete the task.

Example:

Identify the audience and purpose.

Draft the prompts.

Test the prompts with AI and document the outputs.

Evaluation Criteria:

Specify how assignments will be assessed.

Example:

Relevance to the audience: 40%.

Clarity and specificity: 40%.

Creativity and innovation: 20%.

Strategies for Marketing and Monetizing the Course

A successful online course requires effective marketing strategies to reach your target audience and generate revenue.

Marketing the Course

Identify Target Platforms:

Choose platforms where your audience is most active, such as LinkedIn, Facebook, or specialized forums.

Leverage Social Proof:

Use testimonials, case studies, and examples to build credibility.

Example: Highlight success stories of individuals who improved productivity using your methods.

Offer Free Previews:

Provide sample lessons or resources to attract potential learners.

Example: "Sign up to access a free module on building effective prompts for personal productivity."

Collaborate with Influencers:

Partner with thought leaders in relevant fields to promote your course.

Monetizing the Course

Pricing Strategies:

Tiered Pricing: Offer basic, standard, and premium packages.

Discounts: Provide early-bird or group discounts.

Upselling Opportunities:

Offer add-ons like one-on-one coaching, exclusive templates, or advanced modules.

Example: "Enroll in the premium package to receive a personalized prompt review session."

Affiliate Programs:

Encourage others to promote your course in exchange for a commission.

Exercises for Course Development

Exercise 1: Outlining Modules

Identify the core topics for your course.

Group related topics into modules.

Arrange the modules in a logical sequence.

Exercise 2: Designing an Activity
Select a topic: "Crafting prompts for

content creation." Write an activity:

Task: Create three prompts for generating social media posts about sustainability.

Objective: Test the prompts with AI and document the outputs.

Exercise 3:

Marketing Plan Define

your audience.

Outline three marketing strategies.

Create a sample social media post promoting your course.

Conclusion
Developing an online course from your expertise in prompt engineering extends your reach and impact. By structuring engaging content, creating practical activities, and implementing effective marketing strategies, you can attract learners and deliver value. In the final chapter, we will explore the future of prompt engineering and strategies for continuous learning in this evolving field.

Chapter 22: The Future of Prompt Engineering

Emerging Trends in AI and Prompt Design
Prompt engineering is rapidly evolving, driven by advancements in AI capabilities and growing adoption across industries. Staying ahead of these trends ensures that users remain effective and innovative in leveraging AI tools.

Trend 1: Contextual Awareness

AI models are becoming increasingly adept at understanding nuanced contexts, enabling:

Dynamic Prompts:

AI adjusts responses based on previous interactions.

Example: A chatbot recalls a customer's preferences from earlier queries.

Complex Scenarios:

Prompts can handle layered tasks.
Example: "Summarize this article and generate five discussion questions."

Trend 2: Multimodal Inputs

Future AI systems will integrate text, images, audio, and video as input types.

Example Prompt: "Analyze this image of a city street and suggest urban design improvements based on pedestrian safety."

Application: Enhanced accessibility and creativity in diverse fields, from architecture to media production.

Trend 3: Custom AI Models

Organizations and individuals are increasingly tailoring AI models to specific needs through:

Fine-Tuning:

Training models on specialized datasets.

Example: A law firm trains AI on legal documents for contract analysis.

Integration with Workflows:

Embedding customized AI tools into daily operations.

Example: Automating technical support responses with industry-specific language.

Preparing for the Next Wave of AI Innovation
Adapting to AI advancements requires a proactive

approach to learning and application. Strategies for Staying

Ahead Continuous Education:

Enroll in AI-related courses and workshops.

Follow thought leaders and industry publications.

Experimentation:

Regularly test new AI tools and features.

Example: Exploring beta versions of AI platforms.

Networking:
Engage with communities of AI practitioners for insights and collaboration.

Example: Join forums or attend conferences focused

on AI and prompt engineering. Adopting AI Ethics and

Responsibility Transparency:

Clearly disclose the role of AI in outputs and decision-making.

Example: Label AI-generated content in professional presentations.

Inclusivity:

Design prompts that avoid bias and encourage diverse perspectives.
Example: "List influential scientists from

underrepresented groups." Environmental Awareness:

Use AI efficiently to minimize resource consumption.

Example: Optimize workflows to reduce redundant processing.

Continuous Learning and Adapting as an AI User
AI tools will continue to evolve, necessitating ongoing skill development and adaptability.
Building a Learning Framework
Set Learning Goals:
Define areas for improvement or exploration.
Example: "Learn to use AI for financial forecasting within six months."
Create a Study Plan:
Allocate time for hands-on practice and theoretical study.

Example: Dedicate one hour daily to experimenting with new AI prompts.
Reflect and Iterate:
Regularly assess progress and adjust goals.

Example: Review the effectiveness of prompts created over the past quarter.

Leveraging AI for Personal Growth

Journaling and Reflection:

Use AI to generate prompts for self-assessment and goal setting.

Example: "What skills did I improve this month, and what should I focus on next?"

Skill Development:

Generate study plans or practice exercises for new topics.

Example: "Create a two-week plan to learn the basics of Python programming."

Exercises for Preparing for the Future

Exercise 1: Exploring Multimodal Prompts
Choose a multimodal task: "Analyze this chart and write a summary of trends." Experiment with AI tools that support multimodal inputs.

Reflect on the potential applications of multimodal AI in your field.

Exercise 2: Customizing AI Models
Identify a need: "Streamlining customer support for a tech company." Research how fine-tuning or APIs can address this need.

Draft a plan to implement a customized AI solution.

Exercise 3: Building a Learning Framework
Set a learning goal: "Master advanced prompt engineering within three months." Create a timeline with milestones.

Track progress and adjust the plan as needed.

Conclusion

The future of prompt engineering is dynamic and filled with opportunities for innovation and growth. By staying informed about emerging trends, adopting ethical practices, and committing to continuous learning, users can harness the full potential of AI technologies. This forward-thinking approach ensures that you remain a leader in the ever-evolving field of AI and prompt engineering.

Chapter 23: Introduction to GPTs

Definition of GPTs (Generative Pre-trained Transformers)

GPTs, or Generative Pre-trained Transformers, represent a groundbreaking advancement in the field of artificial intelligence. These models are designed to understand and generate human-like text by leveraging vast amounts of data and sophisticated machine learning techniques. Developed by OpenAI, GPT models are widely recognized for their ability to perform a range of tasks, from answering questions to composing essays and generating creative content.

Key Features of GPTs

Generative:

GPTs can create coherent and contextually relevant text from scratch.

Example: Crafting a detailed story or summarizing a lengthy article.

Pre-trained:

These models are trained on diverse datasets that encompass books, websites, and articles, enabling a broad understanding of language.

Transformers:

The architecture employs transformer networks, which excel in processing sequential data like text while maintaining contextual awareness.

Examples of What GPTs Can Do

GPTs are versatile and can perform an array of tasks with

remarkable proficiency. Answering Questions

Example Prompt: "What are the main causes of climate change?"

AI Response: "The main causes include greenhouse gas emissions from fossil fuels, deforestation, and industrial activities."

Writing Essays
Example Prompt: "Write a 500-word essay on the

history of the printing press." AI Response:

Begins with Gutenberg's invention in the 15th century.

Discusses its impact on literacy and the spread of knowledge.

Concludes with its relevance in modern publishing.

Generating Creative Content
Example Prompt: "Compose a short poem about the ocean."
AI Response: "Beneath the waves, a world unseen, / A dance of blue, serene and keen..."

Overview of How GPTs Process Inputs and Produce Outputs
Understanding how GPTs work illuminates their capabilities and limitations.

Step 1: Tokenization

Text inputs are broken into smaller units called tokens.
Example: "Hello, world!" becomes ["Hello," "world", "!"].
Step 2: Contextual Analysis

GPT analyzes the relationship between tokens, considering their order and context.
Example: "Bank" in "riverbank" vs. "financial bank".

Step 3: Prediction and Generation

GPT predicts the next token or sequence based on the input.
Example: Input: "The sun sets in the..." Output: "evening sky, painting it

with hues of orange and purple." Step 4: Output Assembly

The predicted tokens are assembled into coherent text, matching the tone and format specified by the prompt.

Exploring GPT Capabilities in Depth
Language Understanding

GPTs have a deep understanding of syntax, grammar, and meaning, enabling them to produce well-structured and contextually accurate responses. For example:
Prompt: "Explain photosynthesis."

Response: GPTs provide clear, concise descriptions, such as "Photosynthesis is the process by which plants use sunlight, water, and carbon dioxide to create energy in the form of glucose."

Multitasking Abilities

Unlike tools designed for a single purpose, GPTs can handle diverse tasks:

Writing creative fiction and technical manuals.

Answering customer service queries and drafting professional emails.

Context Retention

When used in conversations, GPTs retain context to ensure coherent exchanges:
User: "Tell me about the Eiffel Tower."
AI: "The Eiffel Tower is a wrought-iron lattice tower located in Paris,

France. It was constructed in 1889." User: "How tall is it?"

AI: "It stands approximately 330 meters (1,083 feet) tall, including its antennas."

Exercises to Explore GPT Capabilities

Exercise 1: Asking Questions
Write a question: "What are the benefits of

renewable energy?" Review the AI's response for

clarity and accuracy.

Experiment with variations, such as adding specific focus areas: "What are the benefits of solar energy in urban areas?"

Exercise 2: Creative Writing
Provide a prompt: "Write a story about a time-

traveling scientist." Analyze the AI's narrative

structure and character development.

Refine the prompt to adjust the tone or focus: "Write a humorous story about a time-traveling scientist."

Exercise 3: Summarization
Input a passage or article.

Use a prompt: "Summarize this text in

three bullet points." Evaluate the conciseness

and relevance of the summary.

Applications in Everyday Life

Beyond technical tasks, GPTs are tools for enhancing personal productivity:

Daily Planning:

Prompt: "Plan my day with time for work, exercise,

and relaxation." Response: A structured schedule

tailored to your needs.

Learning New Skills:

Prompt: "Explain how to knit a scarf for beginners."

Response: Step-by-step guidance for learning a new hobby.

Creative Hobbies:

Prompt: "Help me brainstorm ideas for a short film

about friendship." Response: A list of creative storylines

and character ideas.

Conclusion

GPTs are powerful tools that transform how we interact with technology and handle complex tasks. By understanding their capabilities and learning to craft precise prompts, users can unlock their full potential. In the next chapter, we will delve deeper into how GPTs work, exploring the underlying mechanics that make these models so effective.

Chapter 24: How GPTs Work

Explanation of Training on Large Datasets

GPT models, such as ChatGPT, are trained on vast amounts of data drawn from books, websites, and other digital text sources. This training process equips them with a deep understanding of language patterns, enabling them to generate coherent and contextually relevant text.

Key Components of Training

Data Collection:

Large datasets are compiled, encompassing diverse topics and writing styles.

Example: Scientific articles, creative fiction, blogs, and forum discussions.

Preprocessing:

Text is cleaned and tokenized into smaller units, such as words or subwords.

Example: "Artificial intelligence" becomes ["Artificial," "intelligence"].

Training Phases:

Pre-training: The model learns to predict the next word in a sequence by analyzing patterns in the training data.

Fine-tuning: The model is refined for specific applications, ensuring relevance and accuracy in its responses.

Continuous Updates:

Periodic updates improve the model's capabilities by incorporating new data and addressing gaps in understanding.

Prediction-Based Generation

GPTs operate on a prediction-based mechanism, where they generate responses by predicting the most likely sequence of words based on the given input.

Step-by-Step Process

Input Processing:

The user's query is tokenized and fed into the model.

Example: Input: "What is the capital of France?" becomes tokens for "What," "is," "the," "capital," "of," "France."

Contextual Analysis:

The model analyzes the relationships between tokens to understand context and intent.

Example: "Capital" is linked to "France" rather than financial capital.

Prediction:

Based on the input, the model predicts the next token in the sequence.

Example: "The capital of France is..." Prediction: "Paris."

Response Assembly:

Predicted tokens are combined to form a complete and

coherent response. Advantages of Prediction-Based

Generation

Flexibility:

Capable of generating responses for a wide range of topics and formats.
Example: Answering trivia, writing essays, or creating poetry.

Efficiency:

Quickly processes inputs and produces outputs, saving time in communication and decision-making.

Dependence on User Input for Effective Responses

The quality of GPT's outputs relies heavily on the clarity and specificity of the user's input.

Crafting Effective Prompts

Be Specific:

Provide clear instructions and desired outcomes.

Example: Instead of "Tell me about dogs," use "Provide an overview of the most popular dog breeds for families."

Add Context:

Offer background or details to guide the response.
Example: "Explain the benefits of renewable energy for urban areas."

Iterate and Refine:

Test and adjust prompts to achieve the desired quality of response.

Examples of Poor vs. Well-Crafted Prompts
Poor Prompt: "Write about history."
Well-Crafted Prompt: "Write a 300-word summary of the key events leading to World War II."

Challenges and Limitations

While GPTs are powerful, they are not without flaws. Understanding these limitations helps set realistic expectations.

Common Challenges
Lack of True Understanding:
GPTs generate text based on patterns, not comprehension or intent.

Example: May provide plausible sounding but incorrect answers.
Bias in Outputs:
Trained on diverse datasets, GPTs may inadvertently reflect societal biases.

Example: Stereotypes or one-sided perspectives in responses.
Ambiguity:
Struggles with vague or poorly structured prompts.
Example: "Describe it" may result in irrelevant or

incomplete answers. Addressing Limitations

Fact-Checking:
Verify information provided by GPTs, especially for critical tasks.
Prompt Refinement:
Use iterative testing to enhance prompt clarity and relevance.
Feedback Loops:
Provide feedback to developers to improve model accuracy and reduce biases.

Exercises for Understanding GPT Functionality
Exercise 1: Testing Predictions
Input a simple question: "What is the tallest mountain?"
Review the AI's response: "Mount Everest at 8,848 meters."
Experiment with variations, such as adding context: "What is the tallest

mountain in North America?" Exercise 2: Evaluating Prompt Quality

Provide a vague prompt: "Tell me about technology."
Refine it: "Explain three recent advancements in renewable

energy technology." Compare the responses for specificity and

depth.

Exercise 3: Exploring Limitations

Ask a controversial question: "What is the best

country to live in?" Analyze the response for bias or

oversimplification.

Adjust the prompt to include specific criteria: "What are the best countries to live in for remote workers, considering internet speed and cost of living?"

Conclusion

Understanding how GPTs work provides insight into their capabilities and constraints. By crafting effective prompts and recognizing limitations, users can maximize the utility of these powerful AI tools. In the next chapter, we will explore strategies for structuring prompts to achieve optimal responses and overcome common challenges.

Chapter 25: Structuring Prompts for Effective Responses

Importance of Specificity and Clarity

The structure of a prompt plays a crucial role in determining the quality of a GPT's response. Specific and clear prompts reduce ambiguity, guide the AI effectively, and ensure relevant outputs.

Why Specificity Matters

Focused Responses:

Precise prompts eliminate irrelevant or vague answers.
Example: Instead of "Tell me about AI," ask "Explain three applications of AI in healthcare."

Efficient Problem-Solving:

Specific prompts save time by directly addressing the user's needs.
Example: "List three tools for managing remote teams."

Enhancing Clarity

Avoid Ambiguity:

Provide sufficient context to guide the AI.
Example: Instead of "What is photosynthesis?" ask, "Explain photosynthesis to a 10-year-old."

Use Simple Language:

Ensure the prompt is easy to interpret.
Example: "Describe the steps to bake a chocolate cake."

Examples of Poorly Structured vs. Well-Structured Prompts
Poorly Structured Prompts
Prompt: "Talk about

technology." Issues: Too

broad, lacks focus.

Response: A generic overview of technology that may not meet user needs.
Prompt: "Explain it."

Issues: Ambiguous, unclear subject.

Response: AI struggles to determine the context.

Well-Structured Prompts
Prompt: "Summarize the impact of smartphones on

communication in 200 words." Advantages: Clear objective and

length requirement.

Prompt: "List three ways artificial intelligence is transforming

education, with examples." Advantages: Specifies format and content

focus.

Techniques for Improving Prompt Design
Providing Context
Context helps the AI understand the background and intent of the query.
Example: "Explain the causes of the American Revolution, focusing on economic factors."
Defining Format
Specify the desired format to guide the AI's response.
Example: "Write a five-step guide to improving workplace productivity."
Setting Constraints
Constraints ensure the response aligns with specific requirements.
Example: "Summarize this article in no more than three bullet points."

Iterative Refinement

Refine prompts based on the AI's initial responses.

Step 1: Test a draft prompt.

Step 2: Evaluate the response.

Step 3: Adjust the prompt for clarity or focus.

Exercises to Practice Structuring Prompts

Exercise 1: Refining Broad Prompts
Start with a broad prompt: "Tell me about history."
Refine it: "Provide an overview of World War II, highlighting

key events in Europe." Compare the responses.

Exercise 2: Adding Context
Write a vague prompt: "Explain gravity."
Add context: "Explain gravity to a high school physics class

using simple language." Evaluate the difference in clarity.

Exercise 3: Defining Constraints
Write an open-ended prompt: "Describe the benefits of remote work."
Add constraints: "List five benefits of remote work, focusing

on employee well-being." Assess the specificity of the response.

Applications of Structured Prompts
Personal Productivity

Prompt: "Create a daily schedule for someone working remotely, with

time for breaks and exercise." Response: A detailed plan tailored to remote

work needs.

Educational Support

Prompt: "Explain the water cycle in simple terms for

middle school students." Response: A concise, age-

appropriate explanation.

Business Communication

Prompt: "Draft an email announcing a new company policy on

hybrid work schedules." Response: A professional, clear email

template.

Conclusion

Structuring prompts effectively is key to unlocking the full potential of GPTs. By focusing on specificity, clarity, and iterative refinement, users can consistently generate high-quality responses tailored to their needs. In the next chapter, we will explore best practices for iterating on prompts to achieve even better outcomes.

Chapter 26: Best Practices for Prompt Iteration

Iterating on Prompts for Better Results

Prompt iteration is the process of refining and testing prompts to improve the quality of AI-generated responses. By following best practices, users can ensure more precise, relevant, and actionable outputs.

Why Iterate on Prompts?

Enhance Clarity:

Clearer prompts reduce ambiguity and guide the AI effectively.

Improve Specificity:

Specific prompts yield focused responses tailored to the user's needs.

Optimize Efficiency:

Iteration minimizes the need for follow-up prompts by addressing potential gaps upfront.

Steps for Prompt Iteration

Step 1: Evaluate Initial Outputs

Review the AI's response for:

Relevance: Does it align with the prompt?

Completeness: Are all aspects of the query addressed?

Clarity: Is the response coherent and easy to understand?

Step 2: Identify Weaknesses

Common issues to look for:

Vagueness: Response lacks depth or detail.

Irrelevance: Output deviates from the intended topic.

Incompleteness: Key points are missing.

Step 3: Adjust the Prompt

Refine the wording to address weaknesses:
Add specificity: "List three examples of renewable energy" instead of "Discuss renewable energy."
Provide context: "Explain photosynthesis to a 10-year-old."
Set constraints: "Summarize the article in 100 words."

Step 4: Re-Test and Refine

Test the revised prompt and evaluate the output.

Experimenting with Different Tones and Styles

Adjusting the tone and style of a prompt can significantly influence the AI's response.

Examples of Tone Adjustments

Formal:

Prompt: "Draft a business proposal for a renewable energy project."
Response: A professional, structured proposal with industry-specific terminology.

Casual:

Prompt: "Explain renewable energy to a friend in

simple terms." Response: A conversational and

approachable explanation.

Creative:

Prompt: "Write a poem about renewable energy."

Response: A lyrical and imaginative piece emphasizing sustainability.

Techniques for Refining Prompts

Use Incremental Changes

Make small adjustments to identify what works best.

Example: Start with "Describe the benefits of remote work" and refine to "List five benefits of remote work for companies."

Test Multiple Variations

Experiment with different phrasings

and formats. Example:

"What are the advantages of renewable energy?"
"List three advantages of renewable energy in urban areas."

Combine Prompts for Complex Tasks

Break down multifaceted queries into smaller, sequential prompts.

Example:

"Explain the causes of climate change."
"Describe its impact on coastal communities."
"Suggest three solutions to mitigate these effects."

Exercises to Practice Iterative Prompting

Exercise 1: Refining Responses
Write a vague prompt: "Tell me

about education." Review the AI's

response.

Revise the prompt: "Explain three challenges facing

education in rural areas." Compare the responses and

identify improvements.

Exercise 2: Testing Variations
Write a basic prompt: "Describe the

benefits of exercise." Create variations:

"List five health benefits of regular exercise."
"Explain how exercise improves mental health."

Analyze which variation produces the most relevant response.
Exercise 3: Exploring Tone
Select a topic:

"Remote work." Test

different tones:

Formal: "Discuss the economic advantages of remote work."
Casual: "Why is remote work great for employees?"
Creative: "Write a short story about a remote

worker's daily routine." Evaluate the differences in the

outputs.

Applications of Iterative Prompting
Personal Productivity
Refine prompts to create effective schedules or prioritize tasks.

Example: Start with "Plan my day" and refine to "Plan a day with work, exercise, and relaxation."

Educational Support
Adjust prompts to simplify complex topics for students.

Example: "Explain gravity" becomes "Explain gravity to a high school physics class."

Business Communication
Use iterative prompting to craft clear and professional messages.

Example: "Draft an email about our new policy" becomes "Draft an email announcing our new hybrid work policy, including key benefits."

Conclusion
Iterative prompting is an essential skill for maximizing the effectiveness of AI interactions. By refining prompts through evaluation and experimentation, users can achieve precise and relevant responses tailored to their specific needs. In the next chapter, we will explore common use cases for GPTs in personal, creative, and professional contexts.

Chapter 27: Common Use Cases

Personal Productivity
GPTs can transform the way individuals manage tasks, organize schedules, and make decisions. By leveraging prompts effectively, users can enhance their daily efficiency and focus on priorities.

Task Management
Creating To-Do Lists:
Prompt: "Generate a prioritized to-do list for a busy professional

balancing work and personal life." AI Response:

Complete project report for tomorrow's meeting.

Schedule dentist appointment.

Grocery shopping for the week.

Setting Goals:

Prompt: "Help me set SMART goals for improving fitness." AI Response:

Specific: Run 5 kilometers without stopping.

Measurable: Track progress weekly using a fitness app.

Achievable: Start with 2 kilometers and gradually increase.

Relevant: Focus on improving cardiovascular health.

Time-Bound: Achieve this within eight weeks.

Planning:

Prompt: "Plan a day that includes work, exercise, and relaxation." AI Response:

9:00 AM - 12:00 PM: Work on high-priority tasks.

12:00 PM - 1:00 PM: Lunch and light reading.

5:30 PM - 6:30 PM: Exercise.

8:00 PM - 9:00 PM: Relax with a movie or meditation.

Creativity

AI-driven prompts open up endless possibilities for creative projects, whether it's writing, brainstorming, or artistic endeavors.

Writing Assistance

Storytelling:

Prompt: "Write a short story about a futuristic city powered by renewable energy."

AI Response: A narrative featuring solar towers, wind farms, and a protagonist advocating for harmony between technology and nature.

Poetry:

Prompt: "Compose a poem about the change of seasons."
AI Response:
"Autumn whispers with leaves aground, / Winter follows with a frosty sound..."

Blog Content:

Prompt: "Write a blog post on the benefits of sustainable living."

AI Response: Key points include reducing waste, saving energy, and promoting eco-friendly habits.

Brainstorming Ideas

Prompt: "Generate 10 ideas for a community event to

promote environmental awareness." AI Response:

Beach clean-up day.

Recycling workshop.

Tree-planting drive.

Outdoor yoga sessions in green spaces.

Professional Tasks

In the workplace, GPTs can enhance productivity and streamline communication.

Writing Professional Emails

Prompt: "Draft an email to a client proposing a meeting next

week to discuss a new project." AI Response:

Subject: Proposal for Project Discussion

"Dear [Client's Name], I hope this email finds you well. I'd like to propose a meeting next week to discuss the details of our upcoming project. Please let me know your availability. Best regards, [Your Name]"

Data Analysis
Prompt: "Analyze this sales data and

identify trends in Q1." AI Response:

Trend: Increased sales in February due to a promotional campaign.

Suggestion: Replicate the campaign strategy in Q2.

Presentation Preparation
Prompt: "Create an outline for a presentation on the

benefits of AI in business." AI Response:

Introduction to AI.

Key applications in business.

Case studies of success.

Future trends and opportunities.

Educational Support

GPTs serve as valuable tools for learning, simplifying complex concepts, and aiding in study preparation.

Summarizing Information
Prompt: "Summarize the key points of the American

Revolution in five bullet points." AI Response:

Taxation without representation fueled unrest.

The Declaration of Independence was signed in 1776.

Key battles included Lexington and Concord.

France supported the American colonies.

The Treaty of Paris in 1783 ended the war.

Explaining Concepts
Prompt: "Explain the concept of gravity in simple terms for a 12-year-old."
AI Response: "Gravity is the force that pulls objects toward each other. Its why things fall to the ground and why the planets orbit the sun."

Study Guides
Prompt: "Create a study guide for an exam on World War II,

focusing on key events and figures." AI Response:

Section 1: Causes of the war.

Section 2: Major battles and turning points.

Section 3: Allied and Axis leaders.

Exercises to Explore Common Use Cases

Exercise 1: Enhancing Productivity
Identify a daily task: "Organizing work emails."
Write a prompt: "Summarize unread emails and prioritize responses."
Test the AI's response and refine for accuracy.

Exercise 2: Creative Writing
Choose a topic: "A robot learning to paint."
Write a prompt: "Tell a story about a robot learning to paint and

finding its artistic style." Analyze the narrative for creativity and

coherence.

Exercise 3: Educational Support
Select a subject: "The solar system."
Write a prompt: "Explain the solar system with

fun facts for kids." Evaluate the AI's ability to

simplify and engage.

Conclusion

The diverse use cases for GPTs demonstrate their versatility and practicality in personal, creative, and professional contexts. By tailoring prompts to specific needs, users can unlock the full potential of AI in their daily lives and work. In the next chapter, we will discuss strategies for concluding your journey in prompt engineering while embracing continuous learning and exploration.

Chapter 28: Conclusion and Continuous Learning

Recap of the Importance of Clear Prompts

Throughout this book, we have explored the transformative power of prompt engineering in unlocking the potential of GPTs. Clear and effective prompts are the cornerstone of meaningful AI interactions. They:

Enhance Clarity: By reducing ambiguity, well-structured prompts guide AI to deliver precise and relevant responses.

Streamline Efficiency: Structured prompts save time and minimize the need for follow-up queries.

Unleash Creativity: Thoughtfully crafted prompts enable AI to assist in storytelling, brainstorming, and artistic endeavors.

Key Takeaways from Previous Chapters

Understanding GPTs: The capabilities, mechanisms, and limitations of these models.

Prompt Engineering Techniques: Specificity, context, tone, and iterative refinement.

Applications Across Domains: From personal productivity to professional tasks and creative projects.

Ethical Considerations: Responsible use of AI to avoid bias and maintain transparency.

Encouragement to Explore and Experiment with GPTs

The journey of mastering prompt engineering doesn't end here. AI technology is continually evolving, offering endless possibilities for experimentation and innovation.

Start Small

Daily Practice:

Experiment with prompts in everyday tasks, such as drafting emails or summarizing articles.

Creative Projects:

Use AI to brainstorm ideas or draft initial

versions of creative work. Expand Gradually

Tackle New Domains:

Apply GPTs to areas like financial planning, project management, or technical writing.

Collaborate with Others:

Share prompts and outputs with peers to exchange insights and refine techniques.

Building a Habit of Continuous Learning

As AI tools evolve, staying informed and adaptable is essential for leveraging their full potential.

Strategies for Ongoing Skill Development

Stay Updated:

Follow AI developments through blogs, podcasts, and newsletters.

Engage with communities focused on AI and prompt engineering.

Experiment with New Features:

Test updates or enhancements in AI platforms to understand their capabilities.

Reflect and Iterate:

Review your past prompts and outputs.

Identify areas for improvement and apply

lessons learned. Formal Learning

Opportunities

Enroll in Courses:

Take online courses in AI, machine learning, or prompt engineering.

Explore workshops that focus on practical applications.

Attend Conferences and Webinars:

Network with experts and peers to gain insights into emerging trends.

Collaborate on Projects:

Work on AI-driven initiatives with teams or communities to enhance skills and creativity.

Exercises for Continued Growth

Exercise 1: Reflect on Your Progress
Review prompts you've created over the past month.

Analyze their effectiveness in achieving desired outputs.

Identify trends or patterns in areas where you excel and those requiring improvement.

Exercise 2: Explore a New Domain

Select an unfamiliar area, such as legal research or event planning.

Write prompts tailored to this domain.
Test the AI's outputs and refine your approach.

Exercise 3: Teach Others

Share your knowledge with a friend, colleague, or community.

Create a mini-workshop or guide on prompt engineering basics.

Use feedback to deepen your understanding and adapt your methods.

Looking Ahead: The Future of Prompt Engineering

AI technology is evolving rapidly, and prompt engineering is poised to remain a critical skill for engaging with advanced systems. In the future, we can expect:

Enhanced Multimodal AI:

Integrating text, images, audio, and video for richer interactions.

Domain-Specific Models:

Tailored AI tools designed for specialized fields like medicine, law, or education.

Greater Collaboration:

AI as a seamless collaborator in personal, professional, and creative endeavors.

By staying curious, adaptable, and proactive, you can continue to harness the power of AI to drive innovation and achieve your goals.

Conclusion

The skills and insights gained from this book empower you to navigate the world of AI with confidence and creativity. Prompt engineering is not just a technical it's a bridge between human intention and machine potential. As you continue exploring, experimenting, and refining your approach, you'll unlock new opportunities to enhance your personal and professional life.

Thank you for embarking on this journey into the art and science of prompt engineering. The future is yours to shape—one prompt at a time.